How *Horses* Feel and Think

Marlitt Wendt

How *Horses*
Feel and Think

Understanding Behaviour,
Emotions and Intelligence

Copyright © 2011 Cadmos Publishing Ltd,
Richmond, UK
Copyright of original edition © 2009
Cadmos Verlag GmbH, Schwarzenbek, Germany
Design: Ravenstein + Partner, Verden
Setting: Das Agenturhaus, Munich
Cover photograph: Christiane Slawik
Content photos: Christiane Slawik
Drawings: Maria Mähler
Translation: Dr Thomas Ritter
Editorial of the original edition: Anneke Bosse
Editorial of this edition: Christopher Long
Printed by: Westermann Druck, Zwickau

Printed in Germany

ISBN 978-0-85788-000-0

CONTENTS
How *Horses* Feel and Think

CONTENTS

How *Horses* Feel and Think

A Journey of Discovery into Equine Psychology

Have you ever wondered what it would be like to see the world through the eyes of another person, just for a day? How do they experience their emotions? Do they see colours like I do? How does their smile feel? Well, what would a day in the emotional life of a horse be like? An exciting thought experiment!

Of course there are limits to how far you can explore the experiential world of another being, especially of another species. Yet, by now, so many insights have been gained into the structure of the horse's brain, into its hormonal regulatory system, into learning behaviour and many other areas of equine life that had previously been inaccessible to us, that we can at least get a glimpse of this strange world. As our knowledge of science and animal physiology develops, it is becoming clear that the brains of all mammals resemble each other a great deal with respect to their basic structure and functions. Differences between the equine brain and the human brain certainly do exist, but they are a matter of degree rather than of basic principle. However, we should not make the mistake of humanising horses, but instead must accept their unique character traits and emotional idiosyncrasies as the heritage of their wild ancestors.

In addition, every horse has its own personality as a wonderful creature with its own unique world of experience. We will see how multi-faceted its thoughts and emotions have to be. The explanatory models of the traditional riding manuals regarding behaviour are not even remotely adequate to do justice to the nature of the horse.

As a horse lover and behavioural biologist, I want to use this book to build a bridge between the world of scientific research and the equestrian world, using today's scientific insight to present the natural rights and needs of the horse. Current research findings and explanatory models from behavioural biology help us to understand many interesting phenomena of equine life. I want to let you participate in the variety of studies and the thoughts of other researchers, and to give you a first insight into equine psychology.

But there is infinitely more to learn here. Therefore, embark on a journey of discovery! Let yourself be inspired by the texts, examine the photos closely and gather as much information as possible. Beyond this, there is only one being that can help you to get to know the personality of the horses: the horse itself!

Let us now delve into the fascinating world of horses – perhaps we will see it with somewhat different eyes afterwards.

Marlitt Wendt, February 2009

The Ethology and Evolution of the Horse

Before addressing individual equine learning and living experiences, I want to give an overview of the nature of the horse and the methods of behavioural biology. Horses behave more or less the same way today as their ancestors have always done, in the ways which have proved most useful in nature. Even domestication by man has not been able to change this. Ethology, the science of behaviour, can help us understand the horse's needs better and to participate in its experiential world. For this purpose we have to consider our means of influencing the horse, as well as its natural potential: Every horse is a unique individual, a product of its genetic heritage as well as its environment. Horses are born with certain behaviours, while others are acquired through life experiences. Behavioural science sums this construct up in the term 'nature and nurture', making it clear that both areas have a significant influence on the horse's personality.

What is Behaviour?

At first sight, the question might seem trivial – however, 'behaviour' is a central term and actually quite difficult to define, as it has many levels of interpretation. A grazing horse is exhibiting a behavioural pattern every bit as complex as a horse that is galloping, playing, or doing the piaffe. Such activities are always compounds of a variety of interacting mechanisms, and when evaluating a behaviour, all observable physical activities should be taken into consideration. Depending on the complexity of the behaviour, there may be an incredibly large number of physical features and changes. Take the example of the walk, for instance: how are the individual limbs moving, precisely? What is the rest of the body doing? Have you really considered every part of the body, all the muscles, and the surface of the skin? What breathing frequency can be observed? What is the expression of the eyes? In addition, we can describe the presumed purpose of the horse's actions. Where is it going? What does its facial expression say? Many interpretive elements are entering the equation

When we observe horses in a pasture, we can study the range of their possible behaviours – all we have to do is pay close attention.

here. It is the question 'Why?' that especially represents one of the central issues in behavioural science, and it can be answered on many very different levels.

Tinbergen's Questions

Nikolaas Tinbergen is considered one of the foremost behavioural scientists of the 20th century. Together with Konrad Lorenz and Karl von Frisch, he was awarded the Nobel Prize for Medicine in 1973. Tinbergen developed the dominant theory of modern behavioural biology, which became known as '„Tinbergen's Questions', and which deals with the causes, functions, individual development, as well as the evolutionary development of behaviour. According to this elementary theory, there are four essentially equally important levels of answering any question we can ask about a horse's behaviour: causality, functionality, individual development and collective evolutionary development.

Let's take the example of a spooky horse, and answer Tinbergen's questions:

● The question of causality. You can initially answer this question on the level of the direct, immediate cause. A horse spooks because it has sensitive sensory organs that can send nervous impulses to the brain very quickly and lead to an immediate reaction.

● The question of functionality. Spooking gives our horse an acute survival advantage. It is able to react immediately to potential dangers and to protect its own life through flight.

● Spooking therefore fulfils a function that is necessary for survival in the horse's natural environment.

● The question of the individual development. Every horse will have observed the important ability to spook in its own individual developmental history, its life story, by observing its mother and other herd members, and will have learned this behaviour to an individually varying degree.

● The question of the collective evolutionary development. Spooking has furthermore proven to be an elementary behaviour in the horse's evolutionary development. For millions of years, the ancestors of our modern horses had to evade dangerous predators. Our modern horses are thus the direct descendants of extremely spooky quadrupeds that were able to ensure their survival as a species based on this behavioural structure. We should always keep this in the back of our mind when we complain about the excessive spookiness of our horses, or when we make fun of it.

Instincts in Horses

You could translate the term 'instinct' literally as 'natural urge'. An instinct refers to the inner, unknown impulses behind an animal's behaviour that an observer can witness. Colloquially, we call behaviour 'instinctive' when it happens spontaneously, 'from the gut', without conscious deliberation. For many years, behavioural science was based on what is called instinct theory: an instinctual movement was supposed to be the result of an animal's spontaneously arising inner readiness to act, which is triggered by a key stimulus once it reaches a specific stimulation threshold. In the widest sense, we understand instinctive behaviour to mean the horse's typical, innate

Horses are not just 'instinct machines' – their actions are the results of complex interactions between emotions, experiences, and thought processes.

behaviour. By today's scientific standards this view is outdated, as these simple basic assumptions cannot stand up to the new neurobiological explanatory models. A horse acts in much more complex ways and has to be considered a personality, not an 'instinct machine'. The assumption that horses always act according to a simple stimulus-reaction principle neglects the fact that every behaviour consists of the interaction between emotional states, previous individual experiences, and conscious thought processes, as well as the individual, highly specific situation.

Ethology and Psychology Go Hand in Hand

Until the 1960s, only the 'nature' aspect of the 'nature and nurture' combination was considered relevant to classical horse researchers. They predominantly studied horses in their natural environment and presented their arguments mainly from the point of view of evolutionary history. It was only with the incorporation of the innovative approach of psychology, which focuses on the 'nurture' aspect by researching the development of individual behaviour and the learning processes, that a new dynamic entered equine ethology.

In modern behavioural biology these two explanatory models are now inseparably inter-woven, in order to be able to grasp the horse's behavioural repertoire in its totality. Every sentient being's personality represents the sum of innate and learned elements, which interact constantly. For instance, the innate behaviour of a foal triggers a certain behavioural response from the mother, from which the foal in turn learns something which informs his future behaviour.

Modern equine researchers speak of a model of 'nature via nurture'. There are genetic traits that are switched on only after the individual has had the appropriate experiences. Both horses and humans, for example, are born with the ability to see, being equipped with eyes and the necessary nervous system. But if the exterior stimuli were missing, if we grew up in complete darkness, our vision would never develop. We would be functionally blind, although born with all the physical prerequisites for eyesight.

Modern equine research studies the inter-action of innate and learned behaviours. This requires the statistical evaluation of as much comparable data as possible. An isolated observation by a horse-owner cannot produce a generalised statement about equine behav-iour – no matter how interesting and unusual it may be. In today's ethology it is especially the traditional understanding of the herd and its hierarchy, the horse's ability to learn, as well as friendships in groups of horses, that are the centre of attention, because many traditional ideas about horses have long since

been disproven in these areas, as we shall see throughout the book.

A Brief Excursion into Evolutionary Biology

When we think of the term 'evolution', we typi-cally think of the science of genetic relationships between species. The various phenotypes of animal and plant species have evolved continu-ously over millions of years. Explaining, among other things, the relationship between the horse's behaviour and its environment, Charles Darwin's and Alfred Russell Wallace's theories on the origin of species are some of the most important aspects of evolutionary theory. Almost simultaneously, both proved impressively that the individuals of a population differ slightly from each other, and that small variations, a certain variability in the phenotype, are passed on to their descendants. Nowadays of course we know about the existence of genes as the carriers of inherited information. It is the genes that make the long evolutionary processes down to the horse, and indeed to us humans, unam-biguously explicable.

Ever since the beginning of life on earth, more individuals were born of all species than their various habitats could support. Therefore, they had, and still have, to compete for the existing resources and the transmission of their own genes. Natural selection, i.e. the pressure that differing environmental circumstances impose on each individual, leads to a thinning of the population. Those who meet this selective pres-sure most successfully leave the most offspring behind, and transfer their genetic material into

the future. A population changes over many generations in such a way that it retains only the traits of those individuals that were adapted best to their environment. In horses, their impressive speed and endurance can be seen as a selective advantage, because the slower specimens were more likely to fall victim to predators, and their genetic material disappeared for ever.

The sequence of the horse's ancestry, which is very well documented through extensive fossil finds, is considered the epitome of evolutionary theory. The horse has evolved, over a period of approximately 60 million years, from the forest-dwelling and rather antelope-like eohippus to merychippus (a herd animal that lived in the steppe 20 to 25 million years ago), to pliohippus, which was structurally very similar to the horse (6 to 12 million years ago), and to our modern equus caballus.

It was only during the last 5000 years that humans have exercised a substantial influence on the development of the horse. This process of keeping and breeding animals in captivity is called domestication. Humans selected specific traits among the original subspecies of the horse and bred different breeds, depending on the nature of the task for which they were used, or according to subjective ideas of beauty, by selectively breeding from particular parent animals, whose genes were then passed on to future generations.

The horse has always been a herd animal. Furthering the understanding of the complexities of hierarchy is one of the main tasks of today's equine behavioural researchers.

Development
of Behaviour
and Personality

In order to understand the personality of a horse, we first have to examine and understand the original aspects of its life that were not influenced by humans. Essential character traits are formed during the first days, weeks and months of its life. We should carefully consider at what time the contact between humans and the newborn foal should take place, and how intense it should be, so that the horse matures into a stable individual who trusts humans.

It is also paramount to look at the horse as a member of a community, since in nature horses live in herds – not exclusively, but in most cases. Herd life has various advantages. Many eyes will see more than one pair. Together, it is easier to fend off enemies, and every animal can benefit from the experience of the others in case of an emergency

As we shall see, equine group dynamics are far more complex, and more similar to the human understanding of roles than hitherto assumed. We can therefore look forward to new scientific discoveries. In the meantime, we should throw overboard the long outdated and overly simplistic explanatory models. Not everything in the horse's life revolves around rank and status, either. In nature, relationships are constantly in flux.

Life Begins

Right after the birth, the mother is the first attachment figure for the newborn foal. This is where important switches are set for its future life. If the mother accepts the foal lovingly, it will have a more relaxed start in life than a foal that immediately has to experience the feeling of rejection. Thus, we do horses an invaluable favour by only breeding mares who are able to accept their foals and to care for them.

The first phase in the foal's life is the so-called 'imprinting' phase. Horses are precocial animals: foals are sufficiently developed at birth to be able to stand up, to run, and to follow their mother shortly afterwards. Since horses are born so well developed, one can notice distinct character traits within the first hours of life. For example, there is

Here is where the switches are set for an entire lifetime: a loving mare offers the best conditions for the foal to explore the world trustingly.

the little daredevil, and then there is the dreamer, who takes a little longer for everything. The first hours are very important for the bond between mother and foal. During this time, mothers generally keep other herd members away from their foal, because this is where an inextinguishable foundation for a close motherchild relationship is formed. The foal is imprinted on the mother during this phase. The mother (or any other large, moving object) becomes the object that the foal turns to, whose protection it seeks, and whom it follows. This is how the term 'follow imprinting' was coined, although foals are certainly not always found behind their mothers, but often run ahead. Equally, the mare will bond closely to her foal, take in its scent and explore its body intensely.

In order to familiarise the horse with humans, one can start with the first little training exercises during the so-called socialisation phase. During this phase a sentient being learns what is 'normal', what is considered 'proper behaviour', and what isn't. Foals are very open to new experiences during this period. Just like human children, baby horses learn on the one hand by experimenting and through trial and error, and on the other hand by imitating grown-ups. Horses form their first friendships during this phase of their life, they develop a sense of social relationships, and learn to pursue their own goals. If they have little or no contact with other horses during this important phase, they will have trouble reading them later on. Some horses struggle their entire life, because they had no other social contacts beside their mother during their first months. As a result, they can neither develop a sense for other personalities, nor mature into a secure character themselves.

Imprint-Training – yes or no?

Marketed as a ground-breaking method of early foal handling, Robert Miller's so-called Imprint-Training has been imported from the US to Europe in recent years. According to this method, the newborn foal is touched everywhere on the body immediately after birth, and it is held until it no longer shows any resistance. It is furthermore sensitised for being touched in places that are important for riding, such as the back and the sides, where the rider's leg will be later on. All of this is supposed to create an especially obedient horse and to nip any problems in the bud.

Reality, however, often looks very different. Because it interferes massively with the natural imprinting process by the mother, Imprint-Training can lead to a false imprinting that later prevents the foal from perceiving itself correctly as a horse, to a trauma or state of shock, or at least to a very deep-seated initial sense of insecurity. Since the foal is being restrained, this method can by no means be considered force-free. What is significant, furthermore, is the aspect of over-stimulation. The human over-taxes the young horse through a multitude of impressions in order to demonstrate his/her superior power.

Horses have a right to a healthy, normal personality development that should not be interfered with on such a massive scale. In addition, studies have shown that no advantages can be detected in imprint-trained foals compared to less invasively raised horses.

This process is irreversible, which means that this time never returns once it has passed. This does not mean that the horse cannot learn good social behaviour later in life, but it will find it more difficult than during the phase that is designed for it by nature. A similar thing applies to children who are raised bilingually, as opposed to adults who are learning a foreign language. While children pick up a new language subconsciously, as a matter of course, without having to actively learn it, it is much more difficult to learn a new language later on, and requires much more self-motivation.

Handling a foal lovingly without ever overtaxing it lays the foundation for the development of a people oriented horse personality.

Young stallions are often raised together. A mixed herd with animals of diverse age groups is better for the development of the young horse.

Weaning – A Common Trauma

In nature, a mother nurses her foal for almost an entire year, usually until just before the birth of the next foal, the following year. The foal gradually becomes more independent, takes longer 'trips', and returns less frequently to its mother. However, it stays in touch with its mother and its siblings, and does not complete its process of separation until a few years later. It thus matures slowly into an independent personality, not unlike humans do.

By contrast, the life of a typical foal in human care is different nowadays: after only about six months foals are separated abruptly from their mothers. From one day to the next they are left to their own devices and often have to switch to a completely different group of horses. Many foals find this highly stressful: the sickness rate among them is above average, and they develop the first behavioural issues, such as cribbing or weaving. It is especially detrimental if other areas of life are being changed also, for instance if there is a change in the stabling or paddock arrangements, or if the feed is changed from summer pasture to a winter feed.

The common practice of keeping youngsters of the same age together in groups is likewise not recommended – it's like a kindergarten without a kindergarten teacher. There is nobody who can assume a protective, mediating, or regulating role. Strong foals in particular often become very aggressive and learn to impose their will ruthlessly on the others. Weaker individuals can be pushed aside by the large numbers, unable to stand up for themselves. It would be better to keep mixed herds with animals of all ages, so that the youngsters can find playmates of the same age, as well as experienced horses from whom they can learn.

Another important step in the life of a young horse is sexual maturity. When the hormone production is increased for the first time, the horse's entire behaviour and with it its life and personality, change for ever. The sexual hormones determine not only the typical behaviours for selecting partners, but also sexual behaviour and later the behaviour towards their own offspring.

The Misunderstood Hierarchy

In the past, it was believed that the stallion is the uncontested leader of his herd, and that he can be thought of as the undisputed alpha animal – hence the term 'lead stallion'. Later however it became obvious that the role of individual mares is at least as important as that of the stallion. This led to the development of the term 'lead mare' and the concept of a strict 'division of labour' between the genders.

But what is an alpha animal, anyway? Until the middle of the 20th century the hierarchy in a herd was believed to represent a 'pecking order' that, once established, never changed. There was supposed to be a so-called alpha animal that dominates the other animals. This was thought to be the most aggressive one, which enjoyed the most privileges, but also had the most 'duties' to perform. Beneath this individual, the entire group was assumed to form a chain, down to the so-called omega animal, the weakest, least relevant 'whipping boy'. Each animal would have its place, its clear rank within the group. Alpha would be dominant over everybody else, beta over everyone except alpha, omega would not be dominant over anybody. That was a simple, but based on today's understanding also an incorrect, or at least incomplete view of reality.

Back then, only competing behaviours were taken into consideration for the calculation of a horse's rank, since they are the most conspicuous actions among horses. From this point of view, the stallion appeared to be the most aggressive animal in many herds. However, a 'leadership personality' also has to be accepted and confirmed in its rank by the members of the group. When you include submissive behaviours, such as the calming signals, with

There is no linear 'pecking order' in horse herds. An individual who chases another herd member away from the watering hole can still be good friends with it.

which lower-ranking animals underscore the higher rank of another individual, the stallion may frequently remain the most aggressive animal in a herd, but when it comes to matters of where to migrate or where to sleep, the herd members will turn to a different herd member, namely an experienced mare, who was then called the 'lead mare'. For a long time it was believed that there was a strict division of labour, where the stallion was responsible for defending the herd, the cohesion within the group, and for procreation, while the lead mare was responsible for the direction of the migration and harmony within the group.

In recent years, however, there has been mounting evidence that there are some very aggressive mares, and that the stallion is by no means always at the top of the hierarchy, according to the observations. We therefore have to accept the fact that a herd of horses is a collection of different individual personalities that can sometimes behave in gender-specific ways, but that can also often reflect very individual innate or learned character traits. It is thus a matter of perspective who is 'the boss' in a herd. Is it the physically superior one who can dominate the most herd members, the one who has the most offspring, or the one who can make important decisions? It becomes obvious very quickly that the ranking within the group can be perceived completely differently from the outside, depending on the individual perspective.

In several studies behavioural biologists have furthermore described triangular relationships and even more complex ones as linear hierarchies. You can think of them in terms of: A dominates B, B dominates C, while C in turn dominates A ... Who has the highest rank? Rank thus cannot be an absolute position, but merely helps in understanding a dynamic group structure. Dominance is here a feature that only makes sense for the description of a specific situation involving two animals. No animal is dominant in an absolute sense. Talking about dominant horses that need to be controlled through dominance training is therefore a moot point.

Contemporary behavioural science views horse herds as cooperative communities of individuals. Each horse plays a certain individual role. While tolerating close contact from some herd members, it will keep a certain distance from others. Friendships transcend gender and age. Especially brave animals are more likely to defend themselves and their group than others. Especially sensitive ones may smell watering holes more often – and the others follow them without argument, even if they are otherwise very timid. An older horse generally knows the environment better than a young one. It therefore makes sense for the others to trust this 'wise' horse.

Just like human societies, horse societies don't follow a universally applicable pattern. Yet, every horse knows its position vis-à-vis all the others. It has a status, a 'job', a gender-specific role, and many other traits. These individual positions do have a hierarchic structure and are certainly defended by the individual horse in many

The Herd – Source of Conflict and Oasis of Peace

Like many other species, horses live in herds, in order to fulfil their basic needs effectively, to avoid harm, and to produce as many healthy offspring as possible. The advantages of living in a herd lie in the balanced cooperation with each other. The group offers security, the opportunity to rest, and protection for each individual group member. Suitable breeding partners are also available, so that an animal does not have to shoulder the burden of going in search of them. On the other hand, there are disadvantages, too, such as competition for scarce resources during a drought.

situations. After all, these rankings affect the access to resources that are necessary for survival. It makes sense in nature to recognise the talents and weaknesses of the others, in order to avoid having to fight things out in a conflict.

Friendships for Life

Friendships are especially important in a horse's life. Horses form very close bonds that transcend gender and age of the animals. The position of the mother does not determine the future position of her foals, either. Close friends spend much time with each other, grazing next to each other, dozing next to each other, and swishing the flies out of each other's faces. Especially conspicuous is the mutual grooming, called 'allogrooming', which serves the consolidation of friendships between horses, in addition to conditioning the coat. Horses choose their closest friends individually according to their chemistry, over age and breed differences. Although they are capable of forming new relationships all their lives, one can frequently notice a form of grieving over a friend when they are separated.

In the Realm of the Senses

To discover the world of a different being, we first have to study their sensory perceptions. Many things that animals experience on a daily basis remain inaccessible to us humans. The fact that horses can find a watering hole merely through their sense of smell will forever be a mystery to us. How different would the world be, if we could experience it through the senses of a horse?

We humans perceive our world mainly through our sense of vision. However, the other senses are extremely important as well, and our brain compiles an overall picture from the sum total of all the information that constantly inundates us through our sensory organs. Combined with emotions, this picture makes up our very individual reality. Horses experience a different world than we humans, because they process sensory perceptions that are completely unknown to us. In addition to perception through the eyes and ears, horses possess a highly efficient sense of smell and an extremely sensitive tactile sense. They can feel the finest vibrations through their hooves, and their highly developed body awareness helps them to sort out their four legs. This wealth of sensory sources of information doesn't exactly make it easy for us to relate to the experiential world of horses.

In the following chapters we will therefore focus mainly on seeing and hearing, in order not to exceed the scope of this book and to have sufficient space for a little journey of discovery into the sensory world that is both familiar and yet so foreign to us.

Seeing the World with Equine Eyes

Horse eyes are extremely large. They are among the largest eyes in mammals. We can therefore assume that seeing plays a very important role in the life of a horse as well. The first obvious difference between human eyes and equine eyes consists in their positioning on the head. Our eyes face forward, whereas the horse's eyes are more on the side of the head. This gives the horse a field of vision that allows him almost a 360 degree view of his environment. For a prey animal like the horse this has the enormous advantage that it can scan its entire environment for enemies while grazing. This is the only way to ensure its security while ingesting the huge amounts of food that it needs to survive. A horse in a herd can thus see the horses in front of him, next to him, and the stragglers behind him, all at the same time. How nice this would be for all motorists: the annoying look over the shoulder and the constant mirror checks would be unnecessary.

The lateral positioning of the eyes on the head provides a very large field of vision.

In addition, peripheral vision is very well developed in horses. Their eyes are therefore especially sensitive to motion diagonally behind them. There is a good reason why they are startled so easily by it: in their natural environment it is important that horses notice movement on the edge of their field of vision very early in order to recognise potential dangers in time.

Compared to humans, horses are rather far-sighted, which means that they don't see objects especially clearly that are very close. This is a perfect adaptation of the visual sense to the original living environment of the horse, the steppe, because predators can be easily recognised from a large distance – it is not so well suited, however, to the environment that is shaped by humans. In order to see clearly objects that are in close proximity, horses really need reading glasses.

The very wide field of vision of the horse has a small, but very consequential limitation. There is an area of approximately five degrees which the horse cannot see with a straight head and neck. This blind spot is located in part directly above the horse's back, in other words exactly where the rider is sitting, and has led to many misunderstandings between horse and rider. Just as we can see the face of the child that we are carrying on our shoulders only if we twist our neck, the horse can see the rider only if it turns its head a little to one side. A young horse whose head is fixed with side reins can therefore become easily scared of the rider. It cannot see the rider, until s/he moves his/her legs or wiggles the whip, which can then be perceived as a sudden threatening movement on the edge of its field of vision. Horses can detect movement in this area very well, but they

cannot see especially clearly, which means that they cannot identify the cause of this unexpected movement, so they often react with insecurity. If they are punished for their natural tendency to flee forward, an unfortunate vicious cycle develops.

The second limitation of the circular vision concerns the area directly in front of the horse's head. There is something comparable in humans: When we look straight ahead and move one finger closer and closer to our nose, the finger will seemingly disappear at one point. This peculiarity of the field of vision has the

The horse's field of vision: the horse sees the area best that is marked in green. The white area is blurry, while objects in the red area are in the blind spot. That is why the horse needs to be able to carry its head high enough during the approach to a fence, in order to be able to gauge the jump correctly.

pleasant effect that our own nose is not constantly in the picture. We know that intellectually. To our horse, however, an object may really seem to have disappeared, and it is scary when this object suddenly reappears out of nowhere.

As far as colour recognition is concerned, horses seem to be able to differentiate between several colours. They can see the contrasts between yellow and blue especially well, while various hues of green probably look more like shades of gray. All red and orange hues are also likely to look similar to horses. However, scientists are still uncertain in many areas, and the discoveries contradict each other every few years.

A final important point is spatial vision. We humans can see only those objects in three dimensions that we can see with both eyes simultaneously. That is no different for the horse. It sees some things on its right side with its right eye, and some things on its left side with its left eye. Only objects that are located at a certain distance directly in front of the horse can be focused on by both eyes simultaneously and thus appear in 3D. That is the only place where distances can be judged correctly. There are significant differences between various types of horses in this respect. Many Arabian horses have slightly narrower, protruding eyes. They can see a larger area in three dimensions than many trotting horses, whose eyes are farther on the side of the head.

The Light in Their Eyes

Our eyes are not made for sudden, intense light stimuli – for instance the flashlight of a camera that you happen to look into. For a brief moment, until they have recovered, we are practically blind. Horses have this experience much more often, as their eyes are especially light sensitive. The reason for this is a special layer in the eye, the tapetum lucidum, which also creates the glowing effect of cat's eyes. It improves the ability to see in low light, since it reflects the light back into the eye. Our horse can still see at dusk, long after we are unable to recognise anything anymore. To the horse, this ability has been necessary for its survival, since predators in the steppe also hunt in the dark.

This light sensitivity is challenging for horses in light-dark situations. For instance, they may refuse for no good reason to step out of the dark indoor arena into the sunlit courtyard. Only a rider who has never thought about the different sensory impressions of horses will punish such natural behaviour. Common conflict situations during trailer loading, when the paint on the trailer reflects the sunlight very brightly, can also be avoided altogether. Give the horses and their eyes a moment to adjust, and they will come out of their seemingly unwilling rigidity and follow us again.

The Tone Sets the Mood

Horses have very mobile ears, which they can turn towards a noise or away from it – depending on whether the noise attracts their attention or whether the volume or frequency are unpleasant for them. We can compare this ability to that of a stethoscope that allows a physician to accurately pinpoint the location of a sound within the body. A horse can also move its ears separately from each other. It can thus direct its attention like a directional microphone forward to the unknown path as well as back towards the rider.

Ears that are pointing backward are often misinterpreted: Horses that react like this when being addressed loudly by their human probably don't intend this sign as a threatening gesture, for they are protecting their sensitive ears from the loud, unpleasant noise. This example also shows that you must not jump to conclusions about a horse's mood based on a single physical signal (pinned-back ears in this case). A closer look at the entire face and the overall posture, and misunderstandings wouldn't happen so often.

The horse's hearing is so sensitive that it can pick up high frequencies that are above our own hearing range. According to research studies, horses can hear sounds in the frequency range of 60 hertz to approximately 33.5 kilohertz, whereas the audible range for humans covers 20 hertz to no more than 20 kilohertz. It can therefore happen that a horse spooks at a high-pitched squeak that escapes our ears – and again we wonder why they are afraid of 'nothing' again. Human voices are in a frequency range that the horse can hear very well, but to which it is not especially attentive. Most likely, horses register our voices and our monotonous sounds as an uninteresting 'blahblah'; they probably interpret their owner's hand signals and posture more easily than their verbal commands. That's why some trainers use a clicker, as a so-called marker sound. The metallic sound lies in a very different frequency range to the human voice, precisely in that range to which the horse naturally pays more attention. This noise is furthermore unmistakable and transmits no unwanted emotions to the horse. While our 'Yes!' or 'Good boy!' always

The Cocktail Party Effect

Have you ever wondered why you can recognise your name above the din of a party, or follow your conversation partner without being distracted by the other conversations? Your brain is able to focus your hearing on a specific sound source and to give it your undivided attention. This process is called the cocktail party effect. Certain sounds that we want to focus on or with which we have a strong emotional connection, such as our name, are filtered out of the acoustic wall of sound. Similarly, horses can isolate those sounds from the overall background noise that are important to them personally. For instance, a mare will recognise the call of her foal right away.

Three times pinned ears: These two are threatening each other playfully...
While the two grey horses are turning their ears sideways/backwards out of a sense of relaxed well-being.

This horse is dozing. Its ears are pointing backward in relaxation.

sounds a little different, depending on whether we are calm, distracted or relaxed, the sound of the clicker is always consistent and neutral.

Caution: Stimulation!

There are many other examples of specific phenomena in which humans and horses differ with respect to their sensory perception. Just think of the fact that through their hooves, horses can feel the ground vibrating at the approach of horses or humans. Or take the fleming response: horses can detect and analyse certain scents this way with a kind of second nose, the Jacobson's organ in their palate. A stallion can thereby reliably detect when a mare is

fertile. Horses also possess an excellent body awareness that enables them to control their balance and achieve perfect alignment in space even in the most complicated movements, like the half-pass or the capriole.

We should always be aware that the experiential worlds of humans and horses differ significantly. Horses have to get along in their natural environment, and we in ours. However, where horse and human meet, we should always make an effort to do justice to the manifestly superior sensory abilities of our friends. We must not draw conclusions about how horses see our environment that are based on our own impression of it.

And above all: horses can stay mentally healthy only if their sensory input is neither

Even if we see 'the same thing', the sensory perceptions of our horses differ significantly from humans.

too challenging nor too static. We humans can offer constant stimulation to the horse's brain through the way we design their living space. But we should avoid over-stimulation. A horse can be prepared early and slowly for all extraordinary stimuli. It can have positive experiences on a small scale first, and then become used to increasingly greater challenges. We probably would not take a baby or toddler to a fair, then immediately afterwards to a family party, where he is handed from aunt to aunt, and finally to a disco with loud music and bright lights.

Sensory organs are the window onto the world, so to speak, the connection between the brain and the exterior world. Through the sensory organs, information reaches the brain, where it is processed and has an immediate impact on the emotions. As surprising as the differences are between the horse's sensory perceptions and our own, we will see in the following that the emotional world of our horses can also be very different, and yet it can sometimes be very similar to our own.

The 'second nose', Jacobson's organ, is at work here.
By fleming, horses can take in and analyse scents intensively.

Emotions –
an Alien World

How can we grasp the emotions of our horse, when so often we cannot even understand our own, much less those of another human being? We cannot look inside the horse's head. However, thanks to modern behavioural biology, we can study the emotional world of other species. In humans it is now possible through magnetic resonance tomography to show which areas of the brain are active while the test persons look at certain objects or have certain emotions. Equine brains are built fundamentally very similar to human brains. We can therefore assume similar functions and emotions, within certain limits.

For many years, researchers studied mainly the mind, conscious thought in human and in animals, since this area was easier to grasp. Yet emotions are one of the most important triggers for action. Horses can feel fear, anger, joy or pain, just like we do. They react with these emotions to external influences, in order to adapt their behaviour to the current situation. Thoughts and emotions, the conscious and subconscious parts of the brain, are inextricably linked. They both contribute to the decision-making process. Nobody can ignore one of the two parts. The mind and the emotions together form the personality of a horse.

Every horse possesses unique emotional 'hard wiring' that shapes its character. The horse's individual personality determines its likes and dislikes, desires and fears, and its dominant behavioural patterns. This almost inexhaustible multitude of different equine personalities makes life with them so interesting and attractive, but often also confusing and unpredictable.

Do You Feel It Too?

We may seem to share many beautiful experiences with our horses. But how do they experience the beautiful hack at dawn, or our competitive success, the dressage lesson? Are they happy with them? Or are they mostly sad about their life? Do they dream of shared hours with us, or do they long for a separate life among their own species? How much do they appreciate the clean, practical stabling with the individual box stalls that can unfortunately still be found in many yards? Would they tell us they liked living there, if you could ask them? The horse cannot speak. It cannot verbalise wishes and expectations itself. It is a being that handles emotions and pain very quietly, unlike humans. Its feelings are therefore often simply overlooked or semi-consciously ignored. Sure, we would not like to feel spurs in our sides, but do horses feel exactly like we do?

As long as the horse seems to be physically healthy and the owner isn't outrightly abusive, the animal's feelings are not normally considered important. Many owners retain old thought structures and ignore the emotions of their horses, simply because they know no feasible way out of their own behaviour. Riding is a traditional sport. Unfortunately, this sport is often carried out literally 'on the backs of the horses', to their psychological and physical detriment.

The Origin of Emotions

Emotions are physical reactions to external events. They are either innate or are learned during the course of a lifetime, and they serve to harmonise the needs of the body with external circumstances of life. This arbitration mechanism enables the body to produce a behavioural reaction that is optimally geared towards fulfilling its own needs and goals. This is a sober, rather scientific explanation of the complex phenomenon known as 'emotion'. In reality, there is much that we do not understand concerning the emotions, and formulating a general definition is problematic. Of course we can name our own feelings. For instance, fear, rage, or happiness are emotions that probably everyone can relate to, and that horses most likely feel as well. In many animal species, the same physical processes occur in the brain when they are experiencing negative emotions like fear, anger, or pain, but also positive emotions such as joy. In all mammals, these 'basic emotions' are seated in an evolutionarily very old part of the brain, the brainstem and the amygdale, which is located in the so-called limbic system. Since all these emotions unfold through the same chemical

A beautiful autumn hack - how much are the horses enjoying it? A question that only those who have learned to interpret the horse's subtle signals can answer.

and physical processes in mammals, it can be assumed that they are experienced similarly by humans and animals.

The brainstem and the limbic system subconsciously regulate bodily functions that are vital for survival, without any contribution from the conscious mind. If these brain areas are strongly stimulated through emotions, other regions of the brain can only work to a limited degree, as they are blocking each other. This is one of the reasons why horses and people are very limited in their ability to make conscious decisions while in the grip of powerful emotions. Neither horses nor humans can learn if they are very scared. It is therefore nonsense to continue exposing a scared horse to a scary situation, in the hope that it will learn to deal with its fear. Constructive learning successes are simply impossible for the horse's brain in this situation. The advantage of this system lies in the ability to take immediate action for survival in case of danger. Each individual emotion consists of a series of physiological changes, thoughts and subconscious reactions, and fine nuances of facial expressions and postures. For instance, the emotion of fear, which we will discuss later on, probably has a very similar effect on humans and horses. Let's assume you yourself are afraid of heights, and your horse is afraid of tractors. Then you would both react surprisingly similarly in the respective situations that trigger the fear response: the heart would beat faster, perhaps you would both start sweating soon, you would remember past experiences within a fraction of a second, and you would see your worst-case scenario before your mind's eye ('Oh no, I'm about to fall!' or 'The monster will eat me!'). Onlookers would be able to identify your fear by the tense posture, the wide-open, bulging eyes, and the dilated pupils.

Fear is an emotion that is necessary for survival, and it triggers similar physical reactions in all sentient beings.

Through creative ideas you can teach horses that are suffering from stress to enjoy joint activities with humans again.

It is the sum of these changes that add up to the feeling, and afterwards it will be difficult to tell what came first, the physical reactions or the fearful thought. This is a complex feedback loop: one can be the trigger for the other, and vice versa. If we take this fact to heart, we can understand why laughter can be therapy for a depressed person. We can pretend we are happy for the benefit of the brain by faking the typical outward expressions of joy (laughter, pulling up the corners of the mouth, jumping around happily) and the typical thoughts ('This is fun!', 'I'm happy!'). The brain will respond to it as to real joy, and we will feel better in a short amount of time. This realisation can be relevant in the treatment of stressed or depressed horses as well. 'Joy' can be generated through play therapy in order to put a smile back on the horse's face, so to speak.

Messages from the Brain

The brain of an animal 'controls' its body with the help of the emotions (in cooperation with conscious thoughts and simple guidance processes). Biologically, every animal should try to reach an ideal state in order to stay healthy and fit and to live as long as possible. In order to be able to recognise what is 'good' and what is 'bad' for an animal, nature has provided it with feelings. Things that feel good (by giving joy or satisfaction) are often good for the organism, while things that feel bad (by creating fear or anger) are usually bad for the animal. That is how the animal will arrive at its behavioural decisions. It will seek the positive and avoid those things that trigger negative emotions. For the newborn foal it is good that the closeness of its mother feels good, giving it a feeling of safety, because that way the foal stays with its mother and can thrive under her protection. In nature, large objects that approach quickly from behind often turn out to be enemies. It is therefore good for the horse to respond with fear in order to protect its life.

These messages from the brain trigger a reaction in the animal's body. We should be careful not to interpret a specific intention into the animal's reaction. Let's assume your horse steps on your toes or pushes you aside. Does that make it ill-intentioned? Perhaps your horse was so excited or anxious that it didn't even pay attention to you – something that happens to us humans, too, from time to time. However, we tend to be more patient with other humans than with our horses. A horse is punished for its mistakes without questioning its motivation. The question about the 'why' is paramount for our reaction, however. Most punishments are completely unintelligible to the horse, because it perceived the situation very differently than we did. A fearful horse in our example will become more timid and nervous, because it cannot understand our reaction.

I don't want to paint horses as the 'better humans'. They certainly can also be furious, possessive, or dominant, and we should not suddenly switch our interpretations from 'our horse always wants to annoy us' to 'our horse is always sweet'. Instead, I want to help strike a balance between an appropriate degree of 'humanisation', without which the exploration of the animal's emotional landscape would not be possible, and the avoidance of an exaggerated idealisation of the animal. Neither extreme is helpful to the horse. In order to really understand a horse, we have to learn to look and listen very closely and to be in tune with its emotions. The following chapter on expressive behaviour of horses gives us many hints about their emotions and motivations.

Look, listen, feel. This way we can get an insight into
the emotional world of our horses.

The Horse's Language as an Expression of Emotions

Biologists refer to any form of communication as language, which utilises symbols for the transmission of information and for the expression of moods. In many animal species and also in us humans, communication consists of acoustic as well as visual and chemical signals. Each signal must have a clearly defined meaning, and communication can succeed only when both communication partners are able to interpret the other's expressive range. Whereas humans tend to communicate verbally, horses express their emotions and needs through a complex body language. Only an exchange of information as equals, only a true dialogue can form the basis of a friendship. But unfortunately many horses are subject to an endless monologue. They constantly hear: 'We're going over there', 'Stop it!' or 'Go faster!' Such one-sided interactions have no place in a partnership. Only if you let the horse 'get a word in', can you speak of a true partnership. We must therefore learn to understand the subtle body language of horses. It is the mirror of their soul, and it is the only way they can communicate their desires, needs, and emotions.

The ABC of Horses

Many of us have studied the large 'categories' of horse language. 'Pinned ears' means 'angry', 'fidgeting' means 'nervous', and so on. But it's not as simple as all that, because our horses have many nuanced means of expression.

A horse's first symptom of reacting to a pinched girth certainly does not consist of biting its owner. It has probably been hinting for months at its discomfort without, however, being noticed. Many girt-shy horses show their displeasure when the human brings the saddle out of the tack room. They tense up, their body stiffens,

Pinned ears can have many meanings. In order to understand the horse's language it is important to include the whole face and also the horse's overall posture in the analysis.

and their nostrils contract. Many people react to the horse prancing away or snapping at the rider the first time only with a smack and the statement: 'He is only being rude.' Such riders are generally not ill-intentioned, but most people have never learned to pay close attention to the changes in their partner.

In order to interpret the horse's body language correctly, we need to systematically summarise the large features of its overall posture before coming to the finer nuances. Let's examine the main emotions, fear, anger, joy, relaxation, and their interpretations in the horse's expression first, before we look at the nuances.

Fear – A Powerful Emotion

As herbivores, horses are typical prey animals. That's why they have always needed to be attentive and alert at all times, in order to recognise potential dangers early on. In an unknown sit-uation, the body of a fearful horse stiffens, its musculature is tense, all movements look nervous and disharmonious. It usually carries its head high, the tail is pressed down, in extreme cases even pinned between the hind legs. Every rider has probably at least read about the typical fear-face of a horse, with elongated upper lip, a tense mouth, ears pointing backward and slightly to the side, nostrils flaring, and bulging eyes. Further indications of fear in a horse can be sweating, panting, high-pitched whinnying, frequent dropping of manure, and an increased pulse and respiratory rate.

However, it is by no means the case that all these components have to be present in order to be certain that a horse is afraid. The individual

This face has only one emotion written all over it: naked fear.

expressive behaviour of any horse does not always correspond with the 'textbook' expressions. While an extroverted horse tends to prance around, whinny and sweat, showing all the facial expressions described above, an introverted horse is often misunderstood due to its understated behaviour.

This type may appear externally very calm, to an uneducated observer. These horses may show fear only through a slightly pinned tail, tense lips, a tight jaw, and slightly flared nostrils.

Unfortunately, this type of horse seems calm and relaxed for a long time, although it is already suffering tremendously from its fear and, in the worst-case scenario, can suddenly burst into panic with no further warning.

Just because certain types of horse show their fear in different ways doesn't mean that they experience their fears less intensely. As in us humans, fear does not always show itself. Just like humans, horses can be slightly alarmed, they can be afraid, or they can truly panic. We cannot judge the extent of the emotions that are being experienced, especially in the case of a horse. Whether a horse shows an extroverted or introverted fear behaviour depends not only on its individual character, but also on its breed and previous learning experiences. You might say that thoroughbreds tend to be more extroverted, while draught horses tend to be more introverted, but with the caveat that there are considerable individual fluctuations within the breeds. A horse therefore never acts 'right' or 'wrong', because it can only move within its emotional spectrum, and we should accept any horse's fears as a part of its reality and always take them seriously.

This horse is saying clearly: 'Don't come too close to me!'

Faces of Anger

Just as humans, horses can get angry when their wellbeing is disturbed or when their wishes are ignored. They experience anger in varying degrees, depending on whether they are irritated by an annoying fly on their belly, the human is not bringing their feed fast enough, or the rider bounces clumsily in the saddle. The horse shows its anger first with a typical 'threatening' face. We probably all know the pinned-back ears of an angry horse, the pinched nostrils, and the corners of the mouth that are drawn backwards. Beyond that, its musculature seems tense. Depending on the context, it threatens with an open mouth and prepares to strike with a front leg or to kick with a hind leg. In addition, you can recognise the horse's anger by a threatening swing of the neck in the direction of the 'opponent' and the indication of an attack, the so-called 'tackling'.

Unfortunately, the degree of the anger being experienced is often underestimated by us humans. The cute pony face with the fuzzy winter coat will rarely look as menacing as the long face of a warmblood with its long mouth and its large nostrils. But of course ponies are just as serious as warmbloods, when they threaten. These supposedly quiet types of horse are not always ideal family horses that forgive all inattentiveness. If we don't take the pony's anger seriously, we must not be surprised if it bites us someday. What else is it supposed to do to underscore its anger?

Playful Faces and Pouting Noses

Playful faces are unfortunately all too rare! Certainly, many horses wear neutral facial expres-

The Mix Does It!

Most of the time, emotions are mixed and layered. The horse's behaviour is a result of this layering of the experienced emotions. If a horse angrily defends its food against a stronger herd member, because it is especially hungry, it can create an inner compound of the emotions 'fear' and 'anger'. This horse would possibly threaten less aggressively if the fear outweighed the anger, and then it would probably appease the other horse. On the other hand, if it is especially hungry, it may instead threaten vehemently and even enter a fight with the stronger horse. The sensitive balance of the closely layered feelings is responsible for switching from one behavioural tendency to the other. This can even happen within the same situation, because the emotions can directly flow into and amplify each other.

The art for us lies in always interpreting the seemingly contradictory signals of our horses separately. For instance, a horse can pin its ears in anger and at the same time relax its nostrils and mouth. It is thus telling us that it is experiencing an emotional conflict and isn't sure whether it wants to be left alone or interact with us.

A sign of a happy, playful mood: the upper lip that is pushed forward into a 'pouting nose'.

sions when they are being ridden and during their interactions with humans, but when is the last time we saw a truly cheerful riding horse on TV or in the barn? The posture of a cheerful horse is relaxed, the tail is carried normally. It is neither clamped down nor carried straight up in the air. Sometimes it moves almost playfully. It is especially the face that allows us an insight into the emotional world of the horse. The ears are often pointed forward, the eyes soft, the lips and nostrils relaxed. Many horses elongate their upper lip to a 'pouting nose' when they are playing. However, an anxiously agitated or sexually aroused horse can also show an elongated upper lip. You therefore always have to look at the entire horse, before drawing conclusions about the animal's emotional state.

The 'pouting nose' that many horses show when they are being groomed, scratched or massaged can also be considered a sure sign of happiness and enjoyment. The horse's entire body language gives us valuable information about its true emotional state, if we are willing to learn it and to observe it closely. That's why you should not let a horse trainer tell you that the horse is willing and having fun, if its body language says it is not happy, but intimidated and inhibited. Take a look at how many horses really 'dance' or 'play' during exhibitions.

When the Horse's Soul is at Ease

You can see relaxed horses mostly when they are napping or sunbathing. The entire musculature becomes soft. The head is hanging loosely, and one hind leg is cocked. The gaze appears quietly introverted, the ears are drooping sideways, and the lower lip is hanging. However, you have to be careful not to confuse the face of a relaxed horse with a passive, stressed face or the face of exhaustion. A horse in pain looks similar. A relaxed, happy horse has an elastic muscle tone. It feels neither completely flabby, nor exceedingly taut. The elasticity of the skin certainly varies also. We should therefore try to form an impression of the 'normal' appearance of the relaxed horse in the pasture. Only then can we reliably recognise in other situations as well when the musculature of our horse freezes in a split second or if illness or psychological stress is consuming our horse.

Sleepy and relaxed, or sad and introverted? You have to watch the horse's overall behaviour in order to be able to draw reliable conclusions about its emotional state.

The Fine Print of Horse Language

Now we shall turn to the less widely known nuances of the horse's body language, in order to be able to distinguish subtle changes in the horse's appearance more easily. Especially these small, inconspicuous signs can vary from one individual to another, but also depend on the breed and the shape of the face. This fine print in the horse's language is often overlooked, although it is especially important. If we ignore these 'micro-facial expressions', we miss a lot of interesting information.

Facial Expressions in Horses

We can truly read the horse's language 'from its lips'. The mouth and especially the lips can produce wrinkles that vary in number and depth. The lower jaw, for instance, can be clenched when the horse is tense, or it can hang loosely in a napping horse. In humans you can observe too that they 'clench their teeth' when they are tense or focused.

The nostrils can not only flare or tighten, but also wrinkle around the edges. Horses can have wrinkles around the eyes, too, that correspond to human 'worry lines' on the forehead. You can also incorporate the bulging chewing musculature and some large facial blood vessels into the interpretation of the horse's mental state. As the tension increases, the chewing musculature becomes tighter and tenser, while the blood vessels stand out more and more clearly under the skin. The eyes are the most prominent feature of any face. Everybody has an idea of dreamy eyes, a glassy look or an unpleasant stare, although it is difficult to describe these expressions. In horses we can also see glowing, soft and piercing looks if we observe them closely. Horses speak with their eyes, just as we do.

Horses' ears as well as their tail can assume an incredible number of different positions and angles. If we take into consideration that there are thousands of possible combinations of eyes, ears, mouth movements and body language, it becomes obvious that the diversity of expressions is almost endless. We have only started to develop an understanding of our horses and to decipher their alphabet.

Calming Signals

The term 'calming signals' refers to submissive gestures, like the chewing motion that a foal shows to an adult horse, and also to stress signals that a horse uses to appease another horse and probably also to calm itself. Among them are ears that are drooping sideways or slightly backwards, front legs that are slightly buckled like in a foal, with a low head carriage, yawning or chewing with an empty mouth, and licking the lips. These are clear de-escalation gestures. The horse shows these gestures in a stressful situation in order to calm itself down and to put another horse into a milder mood. It is then not willing and cooperative, as some horse trainers claim, but it is indi-

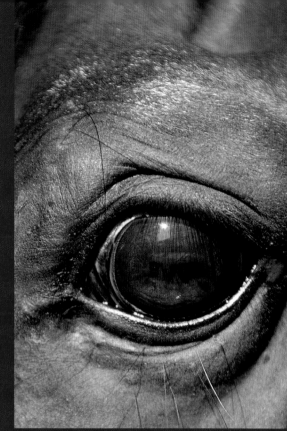

It is worth taking a closer look – then you can see how different the expression in a horse's eye can be.

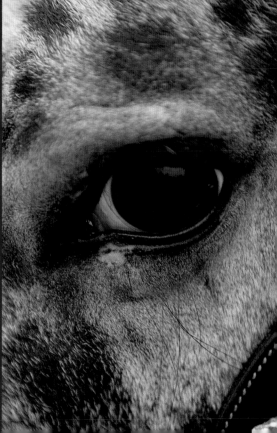

cating that it is overtaxed by a situation, and feels stressed.

Training methods such as the use of the round pen, for example, are therefore by no means free of force, but the horse is showing us that it is suffering a heavy emotional burden. Despite all euphemistic statements about harmony and trust, the horses show us with their unambiguous signals that they are not at all happy with this situation. No training method should make horses feel so stressed that they have to ask us to stop through submissive gestures.

Emotions as Communication Strategies

We have already seen that emotions rarely appear in their 'pure form', but that they are usually a layered mixture of different

Chewing with an empty mouth is a typical submissive gesture that a foal shows an adult horse. This submissive chewing motion can also be observed in stressed adult horses.

emotional states, which can also lead to an internal conflict. Herd animals like horses have developed various communication strategies to show members of their own species or humans how they feel. They also try to gain the highest possible benefit for themselves with these strategies. You can think of this principle as a kind of 'cost-benefit analysis': the 'cost' of a behaviour is the energy that is necessary to drive away a food competitor, for instance. The 'benefit' would then be the satiation of hunger and the resulting prolonged life. The horse's brain will always make new subconscious decisions about the 'costs' and the 'benefits' of a behaviour, and react within a fraction of a second.

All mammals have only four basic different behavioural options in all situations at their disposal. These are referred to as the 'four Fs', and represent all the possible alternatives in a conflict situation: flight, fight, freeze or flirt.

In order to illustrate the underlying fundamental principle, I want to give you a brief example

Constant decision-making pressure: In every situation, every horse can choose one of four basic options for action: fleeing, fighting, freezing, or flirting.

from the human realm. Imagine yourself sitting in a subway and being accosted by a drunken and objectionable passenger. Depending on your personal mental disposition you will tend towards one of the four following behavioural options:

1. You will leave the subway as fast as possible (flight), in order to escape the unpleasant situation.

2. You kick the shin of the hooligan (fight), so that he leaves you alone and you have your peace.

3. You ignore the threat and stare out of the window (freeze), hoping the drunkard will soon leave the train.

4. You make shallow small talk with the annoying passenger (flirt), in order to deescalate the situation and gain sympathy.

These four behavioural strategies apply to horses as well. Every horse will always choose one of these behavioural options, when it is confronted with a new or unaccustomed demand. When a horse experiences fear, for example, it can run away, counting on its fast legs; attack, depending on its own strength and fighting experience; freeze, hoping to lessen the willingness of the other individual to enter a conflict; or communicate in the hope of achieving a non-violent agreement.

Errors in Translation

We have learned: not every horse necessarily shows the typical flight response when it is afraid, but it can choose the other options, such as freezing, communicating, or fighting.

The actually experienced emotion cannot be identified through the chosen strategy! A frozen horse may be experiencing as much fear as one which is fidgeting around nervously.

Unfortunately, people tend to judge a horse's motives too quickly. We should not judge the horse's behaviours, but instead try to understand the underlying emotions and approach the horse accordingly.

Sadly, horses are often punished for not fulfilling our expectations, although their actions are often dictated merely by their fear. Punishing fears is not only cruel and thoughtless, but also extremely dangerous. For even the sweetest, quietest horse may start attacking at a certain point, if we overlook that it is constantly experiencing fear or stress. At some point the desperation becomes so great that the animal has nothing left to lose, and then fighting is the only option.

When the Soul Freezes

Many horse-owners are especially unfamiliar with the behavioural option of freezing. They believe their horse is relaxed and calm, although it is just a puddle of misery that has mentally left its body in order to cope with an emotionally challenging situation. An example from the human experience to illustrate this situation: many people who are afraid of spiders are so frozen in their fear that they are unable to remove the spider – a sign of being emotionally overtaxed. It should therefore be the human's responsibility to avoid

As long as you don't know the situation, it is difficult to say whether a horse is relaxed, when it is standing seemingly quietly, or whether it is frozen in fear.

overtaxing the horse and to prevent an escalation. All four behavioural options are slumbering in each horse. That's why we always have to consider the worst-case scenario. Horses have learned 'main strategies' during their lifetime which they implement in most cases, just like humans. But every horse can also decide on a different strategy in a given situation, depending on its mood and the feedback of its human communication partner. If the human acts aggressively or abrasively from the start, the horse will behave differently than if he appears friendly. The emotional interaction between human and animal plays a decisive role in the behaviour of the horse. Quite a few 'relaxed western horses', and quite a few 'laid-back tinkers' are perhaps not really relaxed, but only frozen inside. The apparent obedience of many horses is often a fear-induced freeze. We should also not be surprised that not every horse runs away from the whip during lungeing, but that many horses attack. These horses don't have a 'behavioural disorder', but they react just as appropriately to a stress stimulus as a fleeing horse.

Insights into the Equine Brain

The performance capacity of the equine brain was horribly underestimated for a long time. The 'switchboard' in the horse's head has turned out to be one of the most highly developed structures on four hooves that evolution has produced to date. All mammalian brains possess the same basic structures. The horse's brain as well as yours consists of millions of little nerve cells that share millions of connections with each other. Even though the horse has a brain that is significantly smaller than a human brain, relative to the size of the body, it is a far cry from the frequently quoted walnut size, with its weight of approximately 500 grams.

The proverb 'leave the thinking to the horses, they have larger heads' slightly exaggerates the problem that arises when you compare the brains of different species: you cannot draw conclusions from the size of the head or the weight of the brain, about the intelligence of its owner. Men have on average heavier brains than women, but they don't necessarily score higher in IQ tests. By the same token, the theory that those animals are supposed to be the most intelligent ones whose brains are the heaviest relative to body weight has become untenable as well. And if the number of twists in the frontal lobe cortex, responsible for thinking, were a gauge for intelligence and brain capacity, the horse would be more intelligent than the dog. It is clearly counterproductive to jump to conclusions from the size and structure of an organ, as to its performance ability.

Small Brains – Large Effect

Nature has equipped every species of animal with a brain that is capable of mastering all demands made by the natural life of this species. Nature gives animals only those organs and structures that are useful to them. So if the horse has a very twisted frontal lobe cortex, it is in and of itself already a convincing indication that it is capable of highly complex intellectual feats. The famous equine researcher Dr Marthe Kiley-Worthington remarked that horses learn very quickly and are often able to store information even after the first trial-and-error round.

We should therefore not measure the horse's intelligence by human standards and dismiss it summarily as low. They may well understand more of our language than we of theirs. After all, the horse's cerebrum forms the largest part of its brain as well. In humans, circa 80 per cent of the brain mass belong to the cerebrum and in

The relative size of human and equine brains in comparison: the human cerebrum (blue) is very highly developed, but the equine cerebrum also outweighs the cerebellum (red).

Pure joy of being alive – who would deny that horses have feelings such as happiness or contentment?

horses, it's around 67 per cent (in guinea pigs it's only 40 per cent). There are significant differences in the importance and size of individual parts of the cerebral cortex. There is a highly active and important region in the horse's brain that is responsible for the processing of information from the nostrils and the mouth. By contrast, human brains are more attuned to processing information from the eyes.

The Source of Happiness

The individual nerve cells in the brain are in close contact with each other through electrical impulses and chemical messengers. Information can be transmitted from one nerve cell to another either by establishing a contact, as in an electrical circuit, or by sending a messenger substance. These messenger substances are called neurotransmitters. The two most widely known neurotransmitters are the so-called 'happiness hormones', serotonin and dopamine. Both play a decisive role in the transmission of information and the formation of emotions.

Humans and animals whose serotonin or dopamine production is compromised feel less happiness, gratitude or contentment. The unimpeded development of all emotions is based on these little chemical messengers, of which several hundred different ones are known so far. We can assume that horses can experience happiness and joy in a similar way to us, since their brains possess the same messenger substances as human brains. The equine brain furthermore shows an area called the nucleus accumbens that is known

as a reward centre. If this area is stimulated by a joyful event, like a relaxed
hack, the horse will remember this event
fondly for a long time. This mechanism is
elementary for an effective learning success, because with the help of the nucleus
accumbens, learning contents are linked
with a positive feeling and permanently
filed away.

Learning on the Limit

The brain requires a lot of energy in order
to be able to work correctly without
fatiguing. However, the brain works not
only when it is thinking, but also when it
has to process a large amount of sensory
input. The human brain uses an incredible
60 per cent of the energy that is available
in the body on a permanent basis. The
horse's brain uses about 30 per cent of its
energy. It is easily over-stimulated when
there are too many incoming impressions,
because the nerve cells take some time to
recover before they are available again.
Next time you go to a show, you should
reflect that your horse doesn't refuse to go
on the trailer out of malice, but it shows
this undesirable behaviour due to the stress
and over-stimulation of its brain that is
caused by the flood of impressions.

When we are asleep, the brain processes
the events of the day through dreams.
Horses also process their pleasant (and less
pleasant) experiences in their dreams.
Horses that are fast asleep sometimes twitch
with their legs, or whinny. Sometimes we
notice that a task which the horse didn't
understand very well the day before seems
effortless the following day. In that case,
the horse made progress in its sleep. By
the same token, we often have flashes of
insight when we are relaxed. Sometimes it
doesn't help to keep wracking our brains to
solve a problem. When the brain relaxes,
other parts of the brain, which may not have
participated in the solution of the problem,
start working and can create associations
that suddenly lead to the solution of the
problem.

The Brain Grows with its Tasks
Connections between nerve cells must be
reinforced or built through life experiences,
starting at birth. If a horse is not stimulated
enough, its brain will not develop. Several
regions of the brain can remain under-
developed for the entire period of the
horse's life, unless they are sufficiently
stimulated during a certain time period,
and they will deteriorate slowly but surely
if they are not used. If a foal grew up in
complete silence during the first phase
of its life, the important time period during
which the region of the brain that is responsible for hearing develops would pass,
and the foal would remain deaf for the
rest of its life, despite being born with func-
tional ears. Horses that have to live in
isolation from other members of the same
species for a long time, can lose their ability
to 'socialise', because the region of the brain
that is responsible for it was neglected. One
could liken the brain of these horses to a

Specifically targeted exercises not only introduce variety into the work, they also increase the horse's learning ability.

computer's CPU with too little RAM, with too few active connections. They are unable to adequately process impressions in their brain and are consequently overtaxed by demands that would be normal for a horse that had grown up more naturally.

Conversely, the intelligence and performance ability can be increased through specifically targeted exercises – a type of 'brain workout' for horses. Every region of the brain should be addressed separately for this, and it should be mostly positive memories that are recorded. Variety in the daily workout can be created through alternating exercises in the arena or on stimulating hacks, and alternating between challenging brain teasers such as circus tricks and relaxation training, along with a species-appropriate boarding situation that offers many occupational activities and opportunities to move. One should also explore new options with older horses to keep them mentally fit.

There is an important difference in the ability to concentrate between humans and horses. Horses cannot simply ignore the emotional area and the region of the brain that responds to sensory input. We humans are a little better at it, but when emotions are very strong, we can observe this in ourselves as well. If we are very nervous before an exam, for instance, we can draw a dreaded blank. Suddenly, we can't remember the simplest things. Our logical reasoning ability is drastically reduced by the experienced nervousness. Our horse will probably be in that situation more often. We should therefore not expect great performances from it when we notice that it is very preoccupied with its emotions – whether these are is nervousness, fear, or anger. It is known that the brain consists of two clearly separate hemispheres, and there is a tenacious belief that horses are unable to recognise an object with one eye after seeing it with the other one. This erroneous assumption is clearly proven wrong by the anatomy of the equine brain alone, as both hemispheres of the brain are linked with each other. Nevertheless, well-respected equine behavioural scientist Evelyn B. Hanggi decided to relegate this myth to the realm of fiction once and for all through an experiment. She covered one eye of a horse and showed him an object before his uncovered eye. After having learned to recognise this object among many others through rewards, the previously seeing eye was covered and the objects were shown to the horse on the side of the newly uncovered eye. All tested horses recognised the test objects immediately. Horses associate things

The way horses learn is context-dependent – which is why it is so important to create a positive atmosphere in training.

and events with their feelings. Everything that happens at the same time is perceived by the brain as belonging together. It is difficult to understand that an emotion should belong with an object. But if we are very honest with ourselves, it is no different for us. We just don't realise it. Many people smile involuntarily when they see a picture of a cute puppy. Hardly anybody will only see the word 'puppy' in the strictly logical area of intellectual thought before his mind's eye. By the same token, many people twitch immediately upon hearing the term 'leg fracture'. We automatically associate pain and suffering with it. It's the same for the horse when it sees us with the feed bin in our hand, or with the whip.

Only some of the many sensory impressions are processed consciously, in order to avoid over-stimulation.

We Live in Parallel Worlds

Humans and horses are caught in their separate individual realities. Our specific sensory perceptions are processed differently by the brain. The brain processes some impressions consciously, while others are overlooked, so that the 'fuses don't blow', when millions of sensory impressions lead to over-stimulation. Based on genetic predisposition, personal experience, and the associated emotions, every horse (and every human) has developed specific filters that decide what is important and what is not. While some of us may always be paying attention to what kind of clothes a co-worker is wearing, others may notice a new potted plant on the window sill, instead.

Each individual possesses an unmistakable perception structure and subconsciously depicts its own personal reality. Depending on the external conditions, a unique brain grows with individual sensory associations and abilities. One valuable part was given to us by our parents through our genes, but another part of the character is engraved into the brain through our life experiences. Perhaps in one person the ability to solve problems was developed, while in another it was only important that the brain was functioning, without ever receiving any support for developing his or her creativity.

It's basically the same with the horse's brain. In the next chapter, I will talk about the creative possibilities to develop the horse's motivation playfully, since learning successes and an increase in intelligence can only be achieved with a motivated horse.

Motivate Your Horse!

Time pressures and performance pressures have no place in interactions with horses, and are toxic to a friendly relationship. The key word 'motivation' is essential for a positive and successful cooperation – regardless of the discipline or the goal.

Motivation can be visualised as the horse's inner mood, which causes it to show a certain behaviour. A horse has an inner readiness to act that is controlled by its personal motivations which determine the direction and intensity of the action. Based on a variety of experienced moods and environmental factors, it will be motivated for one action, but not for another. This dynamic balance is constantly changing, of course. A hungry horse will go looking for food and be highly motivated in this respect, while at the same time not being 'in the mood' for playing with other horses. Later, when it has satisfied its hunger and feels content, things can look very different.

Are You in the Mood?

The motivation of our horses is of central importance. Only if we can convince our horse that it is a great experience to work with us, can we train it without force or pressure. Or in other words, our horse will act according to our wishes only if it sees an immediate reason for doing so. The fact is: a horse sometimes doesn't really want to execute behaviours that it knows quite well, because it isn't motivated to do so. If we want to wake our horse from its well-earned nap and take it into the arena, we have to think of ways in which we can motivate it to cooperate with us eagerly, even though, based on its inner mood, it had planned to do something different.

But why should a horse want to work with us at all? Why do we humans work? Either voluntarily, because we are passionate about something, or because we have to and we have no choice, or because we get paid for our work. An actiyity may thus not be necessarily enjoyable, but the payment makes it acceptable. We will al-

Making the company of humans pleasant for the horse – that's the main job of every rider.

ways be reluctant to perform tasks that don't pay and that are not enjoyable, and we will try to either avoid them or postpone them.

Our horse feels the same way. There are some things that it will enjoy doing. Many horses like to go for walks with their human, because they are curious and interested in their environment. They might go for little walks like that on their own, too, if there were a gap in the pasture fence, because nature endowed them with a certain curiosity so that they are able to scout out their environment in order to find better living conditions or partners. An animal that lacks curiosity would not be flexible enough in its behaviour and would miss out on important opportunities in life.

Mostly it is us humans, however, who bring certain ideas of what to do with our spare time to horses and try to convince them of our ideas. In order to make it worth the horse's while, so that it sees a benefit in cooperation, we have to negotiate a type of 'payment', so that our horse happily executes certain activities despite having no particular liking for them, simply because it expects a reward for them. Horses that are motivated positively, participate with visible joy in the 'work', and they are happy to be able to earn rewards and positive reinforcements.

The Right Work Ethic

What is it in general that contributes to a positive work ethic in our horses and increases their motivation to do something together with us here and now? First of all, all of its natural needs must be met: hunger and thirst must be quenched, it needs a species appropriate living space, other members of the same species, and an occupation. In addition, special foods, cuddling, and sympathetic attention are welcomed as positive experiences, with those things having the highest value that are not available all the time.

Many horses are very curious. They love little surprises in life and need variety in order not to wither away mentally. It is often very easy to make a horse happy in this respect. Something as simple as a new toy or a short walk on unknown paths pleasantly stimulates the horse's senses. This variety has an especially profound impact on our work together, when the horse realises that these great new experiences are connected with our person. We are thus perceived as an attractive and important part of the horse's life. Social contact and sharing beautiful moments between horse and human create the basis for a true partnership.

Inseparable from the feeling of joy is a feeling of security, of being in control of the current situation. In order to be able to experience new situations with a relaxed frame of mind and to accept them as enriching its life, the horse must feel secure in them. And in order to feel secure, it must be successful. Tasks that the horse is asked to perform have to be principally feasible and should match the intellectual abilities of the animal. We will play different games with a yearling than with our retiree. Every horse, young or old, needs clear feedback from us on the success of its efforts. It must not be abandoned during the performance of a task, and should be allowed to participate in the joy of a job well done. It will remember such successes fondly, and this memory contributes to a positive attitude in life as well. We make the experience of success especially easy for our horse, if we ask it

Visit your horse in the pasture from time to time, without making any demands, and simply enjoy the friendly contact.

to repeat slight variations of behaviours that are either instinctive, such as running together, or that have often been rewarded in the past. For instance, we could play a ball game in the outdoor jumping arena instead of the indoor arena. With all the variety, horses should not be overtaxed, of course. Breaks help to consolidate and settle the things the horse has learned, and contribute to relaxation.

Hallmarks of Playing

One hallmark of playing is a lack of seriousness. Movements or parts of behaviours that might very well be serious in a different context are freely combined when playing. Horses thus play with elements of flight behaviour, aggressive behaviour, and sexual behaviour, in loose succession. Play partners often strongly exaggerate the actions, they run very fast, stop abruptly, or bite playfully. The playful intent is clearly visible in the so-called game

Horses are playful by nature and strengthen social contacts that way.

face, with its relaxed facial features and the protruding upper lip.

Young animals in particular play very intensively. They satisfy their curiosity and strengthen their musculature that way. Playing is especially valuable with respect to socialisation. Foals learn to read others, to cooperate, to control their own aggressions and fears, and to develop social bonds that can last an entire lifetime. The brain develops very effectively through playing as well. It is therefore immensely important to give each foal play partners of the same age. Adult horses play much more rarely; some of them don't play at all. Some geldings, however, remain playful all their lives, perhaps because their interrupted sexual development has led to an incomplete maturation.

Positive Learning

The impressive learning ability of mammals has doubtlessly made them a model of success in evolution. A horse always learns – just like a human – from the consequences of its own behaviour. It can thus file away its experiences as either positive or negative. Behaviour that pays off or has paid off in the past is shown more frequently. Behaviour that does not pay off is shown less frequently. We can therefore assume that behaviours which our horse shows frequently must have paid off at some point in time. Even if it is an annoying habit, like pawing in the crossties: it must have somehow benefited the horse in the past, otherwise it would not waste its energy on it. This benefit to the horse has to be discovered. Then you can develop a training plan to make an alternative behaviour more attractive for the horse.

Rewards make learning easier!

How Do Horses Learn?

The horse learns playfully and easily and expands its experiential horizon in a positive sense when its experience shows that a new exercise pays off; in other words, when working with us humans is pleasant. Therefore, whenever we want to teach our horse something new, we constantly have to give it positive feedback so that it knows that it is at least on the right path. This feedback takes the form of either friendly attention or rewards.

This increases the motivation to work for the human tremendously. The horse enjoys being together with us, and finding out which solution it can find for a new task.

The simple fact that a beneficial behaviour is shown more often can be considered a biological natural law that applies universally to all sentient beings on our planet. The human conveys a complete and unambiguous message to the horse through the reward, saying: 'Yes, correct!' The animal thus understands that the human had intended this very solution to the problem and that it doesn't need to try out other possible solutions. It can safely repeat this same reaction every time. It gains security and has more and more fun with the task through the successful repetition. The horse can thus learn without stress, fear or frustration. In this positive basic mood, the horse enjoys learning and learns easily, and it is open for new experiences. Why? Because these new learning experiences are advantageous for the horse, and it always pays off to find out what the human is expecting of it.

Trying out different solutions and getting an unexpected reward is a very stimulating occupation. This speaks very directly to the reward centre in the brain. The relationship between human and horse will improve drastically in the long run, this way. Small presents also preserve the friendship between animals and humans. These presents should represent a true gain for the horse. That's the only way the horse will really enjoy them. Some horses whicker happily during positive training, like when they greet an equine friend.

Demotivating Training Methods

In the long run, horses are demotivated if we constantly reprimand them or pressure them to execute a certain action. It is only a question of the intensity: whether it is a leg pressure, the pinpointed painful stimulus of the spurs, the whack with the whip, yelling, or chasing the horse around. The difference is a matter of degree, but the experience is basically the same from the horse's point of view: It shows a certain behaviour, which is followed by a more or less unpleasant experience, and learns that it is

The Four Possibilities

The human only has four basic ways to influence the horse's behaviour:

- He can do something unpleasant to the horse, in the hopes that an undesirable behaviour is thereby subdued.
- He can end a negative treatment as soon as the horse shows the desired behaviour.
- He can do something positive to the horse with the help of a reward, so that a desired behaviour becomes more frequent.
- He can take something positive away from the horse to reprimand it mildly.

Pressure is unfortunately frequently used, but it is very demotivating for the horse.

better in future not to repeat this experience. Unfortunately, the riding world operates very much on the basis of this method, which is unsatisfactory for the horse, but convenient for the rider.

Two examples from everyday life illustrate this point: when we lead the horse, we pull the lead rope in the direction in which we want to go. The horse experiences an unpleasant pressure on its head, which only ceases when the horse follows. This principle increases tremendously with halters that tighten when you pull on the lead rope, or when you lead with a bit.

And in lungeing, we create pressure with the whip to make the horse run faster.

What happens? Negative stimuli frustrate the horse more and more, and its entire personality becomes clearly subdued. Nobody likes to be constantly told 'No!' Our horse consequently becomes more and more passive and doesn't want to try anything anymore, to avoid the unwanted attention.

In order to motivate the horse in lungeing, the human can run with the horse from time to time and encourage the horse to speed up, through the voice and with re-

Sooner or later, every horse responds with dangerous counter-aggression.

wards. If the positive reinforcements are lacking, the horse will react unwillingly in the future. Every horse, sooner or later, will try to escape the punishment, the rein pressure, or the psychological pressure – serious conflict is thus preprogrammed and there is a real danger of counter-aggression. Remember that, in nature, the tit-for-tat principle often applies. This counter-aggression can be suppressed for a long time out of fear, until it takes the human completely by surprise. Sometimes these horses look for a weak spot in the human system, in order to escape the pressure. Sooner or later they will always discover a moment of inattentiveness. And then, all too often, third parties are unfortunately exposed to danger.

A punishment, even a small yank on the rein, always triggers a stress reaction, and it has been proven by many different disciplines for a long time that stress is counterproductive to any learning progress. It furthermore leads to a deterioration in the human-horse relationship, until the horse only feels reluctance.

Over time, horses become used to pressure, and more and more drastic methods become necessary. You can see this sad phenomenon in the fact that many riders think they need sharper and sharper bits or auxiliary reins. However, this is only the logical consequence of a demotivating training methodology. Many 'modern' training methods work through the manipulative use of punishment in connection with a euphemistic and supposedly force-free horse philosophy. Please consider very carefully whether you want to work with increasingly punitive stimuli, with the attendant risks. If not, then a pressure method is the wrong methodology for you and your horse.

Caution, Trap!

Horses always take note of the environment when they are learning. It is quite possible that a horse does not associate a punishment or a negative experience with its own behaviour, but rather with the people who are present, the location, or the sounds that happen to be audible at the same time. The environment and the people are then perceived in a negative light. The horse consequently associates a certain corner of the arena, for instance, with something negative.

Reward, but Correctly!

We have seen that punishment is not helpful in the learning process. The alternative is called: a reward! With each method of rewarding, the timing of the reward is crucial. A horse can associate a reward (or a punishment) with its own behaviour only if the reward is given immediately, no more than a few seconds, after the behaviour. Otherwise, it doesn't know what the reward was for, which can give rise to misunderstandings.

An example to illustrate this problem: I tell my horse: 'Go back!' It backs up, but immediately afterwards takes a step towards me, because the biscuit bag made such an interesting rustling noise. I give him the biscuit at that moment. What did he just learn? That he came to me very nicely. My horse could not associate the reward with the prompt execution of the signal

'Go back!', although that's what I wanted to reward. In order to indicate precisely the right moment and to let the horse know unambiguously what we want from it, we need a tool which marks the desired behaviour and shows the horse: 'Yes, what you are doing right now is exactly right.'

Clicker training uses the sound of the clicker as a bridging signal for this purpose. Clicker training is an especially effective method of reward learning that was developed on the basis of research in the area of learning psychology. The horse learns during a conditioning phase that a certain

Once the horse has understood its meaning through practice, the clicker offers an option of praising the horse in a quite unambiguous way, which has a motivating effect.

acoustic signal is always followed by a reward. The acoustic marker buys time, so to speak. It can then take a little longer to give the treat, because the desired behaviour was marked clearly through the clicker.

Some apparent rewards are well intended, but unfortunately ineffective. Somebody who ends an exercise when it was well done, who pats the horse's neck at the end of the lesson or gives the reins during a break, doesn't work with rewards, but at best with a decrease of pressure.

The Neutral Clicker

The clicker has the advantage that it produces an easily recognisable sound which cannot be confused by the horse and which lies in a frequency range that is easy to hear. You can also let your horse know across greater distances that it has earned a reward. Of course, we can also use other signals, or a word of praise of our choice. The only thing that's important is that it is unmistakable. If we have decided on a personal word of praise, we have to stick with it in the future, too. However, our linguistic utterances tend to convey not only information, but at the same time we also betray our momentary mood. The reward word 'good' can thus sound very different to the horse, and lead to some confusion.

That is a big difference. A true reward is the addition of something positive in order to satiate a primary, natural need (hunger, thirst, attention) of the animal. In the examples I mentioned nothing positive is added for the horse, or the reward cannot be associated with the behaviour, due to the delay. A horse simply cannot associate the pat on the neck at the end of the lesson with the great flying change 15 minutes earlier. Patting the neck furthermore does not represent a reward for the horse, since it is not a part of the natural behavioural repertoire.

When you watch closely, you can see very clearly from the horse's expressive behaviour which training method it is subjected to. Is the horse eagerly engaged in its work, with a happy expression on its face? Does it want to 'show off' voluntarily? Does it experiment with things? Or does it seem rather dull and bored, because it was trained to be a quitter?

If Horses Could Choose

Next to the right timing and the use of a marker to highlight the desired behaviour, the right choice of the reward plays a key role for the training success. Every horse learns only as well as its human is able to explain to it what he wants.

Not everything that we humans consider to be rewarding for our horse is a true reward from the horse's point of view. Although some horses may perceive pats and praise as a reward under certain circumstances, they are usually not enough. On the contrary, if a horse is has concentrated closely during the circus tricks, it may find the pat annoying, which you

will see very clearly in its body language. Some horses either don't like to be touched in general, or they prefer to be scratched in different places, or harder touches than we humans had envisioned. Take a look and see whether the horse really responds happily to your touch, or whether it withdraws and turns away. Horses love the old 'pat on the neck' much less than we humans often assume.

Carrots and Games

Food is a true reward for all horses, because it satisfies a need that is essential for their survival. Those who claim that food grows right into the horse's mouth in its natural environment, that it is always at it's a horse's disposal, don't realise that the steppe was not characterised by fat green grass, but rather by dry, low-energy tufts of herbs. In order to satisfy their enormous nutritional needs, horses had to be very motivated to ingest high-energy food right away.

The reward centre in the brain is directly stimulated by food, and the chewing motion promotes a general relaxation in addition. Of course every horse has its own preferences in terms of flavor. Some horses are pure 'fun eaters', and would part with a limb for a piece of carrot. Others are gourmets and can only be motivated through exquisite delicacies. Many horses love exotic fruits, such as bananas or mandarins, but also dried bread or oats can be popular variations. It is important to know your horse and its preferences, because training will only

In many horses you can see right away whether they are eager to please or whether their humans trained them to be machines without a mind of their own.

be successful if you know what constitutes an attractive reward for your horse.

However, food is not the only possible reward: You can use anything as a reward that the horse likes. For many horses, playing and movement are a coveted reward that you can use in training. Throwing a favourite ball, a short game of catch-me-if-you-can, a fast run with the human – there are no limits to the imagination. Playing as a reward is often more difficult to apply, however, than a food reward. It is usually associated with wild, ground covering movements. The horse wants to run, buck, rear, bite and tackle, because all these elements are a part of how horses play. Combined with the body mass of the animals, these rambunctious movements can overtax or seriously endanger us. Sometimes our horses get carried away when they are playing and are difficult to stop again. A 'rebuff' in this situation would drastically reduce the motivation, however. In order to ensure our own safety, the play should be ritualised and only involve objects.

But most horses enjoy undisturbed grazing or going for a walk, too, and perceive this as a reward. Always pay attention to whether your horse reacts positively to a reward, otherwise it may not perceive it as a reward, no matter how well intentioned you are. The quality of a reward is always in the eye of the receiver.

Begging – A Problem?

Horses who have internalised a reward system don't beg at all, because they have learned when they can expect rewards, and when not. Only horses who don't know that they have to work for a reward constantly look for food. Often,

Horses differ in their preferences - and for some of them, cuddling with their human is a great reward.

they are in a constant state of excitement, due to an unstructured and unplanned assignment of food, so that they cannot really concentrate on their job. Horses who are experienced with rewards, on the other hand, perform their tasks in a very focused manner and cooperate eagerly.

Should a horse beg anyway, we have to look for the mistake in ourselves, not in our horse. There are a few 'beginner mistakes' that can happen quickly when you try to apply such a complex method as clicker training without knowing enough about the learning psychology of the horse.

The Potpourri of Taste

In a research study, Deborah Goodwin found out a great deal about the different flavour preferences of horses. Some horse-owners may already have known that many horses like peppermints or cherries. But who would have thought that horses can be crazy about fenugreek seeds, oregano, rosemary, cumin, and ginger? So why not bake biscuits with these ingredients yourself? In late summer you can also gather rose hips and dry them for the winter. Many horses like eating these, and they are very healthy and are provided free of charge by nature.

Tips for Quick Learning Success

The horse learns fastest if we create many little successful experiences and avoid failures as much as possible. We should therefore start an exercise on a simple level and increase the degree of difficulty only gradually. For this purpose we subdivide an exercise into as many smaller segments as possible, which should then be practised separately from each other. For instance, for the Spanish Walk, the horse has to learn to lift the correct leg, extend it, continue walking, step actively with the hind legs, and many other components. While you are working on one detail of the exercise, other details aretemporarily unimportant, because the horse can only focus on one thing

Only horses that are constantly fed treats without a plan start begging. Once a clear reward system is recognisable to them, the begging goes away on its own.

at a time. It cannot learn simultaneously to lift the front leg higher and to go more forward. Only when the individual components have been mastered well, can they be assembled into an overall picture.

In order for our horse to be able to recognise our intentions easily every time, we should always give clear, precise and consistent hand signals or commands. The horse cannot understand us if we start the same exercise sometimes with 'go', sometimes with 'walk' and sometimes with 'paso'. Of course, every living being can have a bad day once in a while, and be unfocused or unwilling. If you find that nothing is working today, it might be better to quit for the day and try again another day. The 'back to basics principle' applies here: we confirm the basics in many individual steps first, before returning to the original exercise. This way, we allow the horse to have little successes, which creates security

A clear signal language is important for the horse to understand our intention.

A friendly, relaxed relationship promotes successful learning.

and increases its motivation for the upcoming work. Every work session should end with a good result, because this final exercise always stays in the horse's memory for a long time.

The more your horse practises learning new tasks, the faster and more easily it will learn. It will be able to develop its own creativity and unfold its intelligence.

Brainiacs

Douglas Adams' remark that 'horses have always understood much more than they let on' wasn't meant entirely seriously, but it expresses very accurately the fact that it is much more difficult for us to gauge the intelligence of horses than of our own species. Let's see what horses have told us about their intelligence so far. The term 'intelligence' is derived from the Latin intelligentia, insight. In humans as well as in horses, intelligence refers to an overall cognitive faculty, the ability to recognise cause and effect, and to find optimal solutions to problems. Is the horse an intelligent animal? To answer this question, we have to look at some of the components first that contribute to the overall picture of a horse's intelligence.

Fast Learners

The learning ability, i.e. the speed with which a problem is understood or a piece of information is filed away, varies greatly from one horse to another. These faculties furthermore vary clearly, depending on the daily form, the momentary ability to focus, or the general motivation. It is often also possible to identify a 'talent' for a specific kind of task.

Some horses are true masters in learning complicated sequences of steps, but they are almost hopelessly overtaxed with recognising a specific object. There are horses that can reproduce a dressage test or circus show number without the rider's aids once they have learned it by heart, because they remember the sequence through the music that is part of the performance. Others can recognise very quickly that it makes a difference whether the yellow ball is rolled with the nose, the door can be opened with a swinging of the neck, or a marker on the ground has to be touched only with the left foot. On the

Some horses are very coordinated, but they also grow impatient quickly, if they are not challenged enough.

Horses learn very quickly – whether it is dressage movements or finding the place where they are fed.

other hand, there are horses that have poor fine motor skills. They may easily be able to roll a ball in a large movement, but they have trouble moving it in a specific direction. Some horses find solutions to new tasks very quickly, but they also get bored very quickly, if there are no new demands. They can even get 'angry', if they don't understand a task right away. Being a fast learner can therefore be both a curse and a blessing. These horses make fast progress with new and unfamiliar tasks, but it is often difficult to keep them interested in the exercise. On the other hand, this is what makes working with horses interesting. It is nice that every horse is different.

Memory Artists

Those horses that are the fastest in learning a new task are not necessarily the ones with the best memory. Both abilities exist independently of each other, and have to be considered separately as a measure of intelligence. A well-functioning memory allows the animal to file away, to sort, and to recall information and experiences of past events. It is therefore the foundation of learning. Recorded information is stored in the brain on two different levels of memory: the short-term memory and the long-term memory.

Here is an example from the human world: After reading a cooking recipe, the individual work steps are stored in the short-term memory and are available to us while we are working at the stove. This system, also called working memory, is a kind of 'random access memory' that keeps small amounts of information readily available at any time. A type of 'archivist' in the brain then decides whether the information that is stored in the short-term memory is important enough to be transferred into the long-term memory, or can be discarded. Just as we find we have to look up the same recipe again a few days later, it can happen that our horse seems to have learned to bow very well on one day, but obviously doesn't - remember it the next day. We can avoid this problem if we succeed in transferring the entire recipe, or in the case of our horse the complete movement, into our long-term memory. The transfer between the short-term memory and the long-term memory in the brain is most effective when you heed several important mechanisms: There is a reason why they say 'practice makes perfect'. Information that has been practised through frequent repetitions can be securely anchored in the long-term memory. We should therefore give ourselves, as well as our horses, the opportunity to practiseand become more

A Memory Like an Elephant

The horse's short-term memory often holds information for only a few minutes. But once the information has reached the long-term memory, horses can access it for many years, or even for the rest of their life. Many horses recognise old friends – humans as well as animals – immediately, even after years of separation. Games and exercises are often performed years later without a mistake. Equine behavioural scientist Victoria Lea Voith and her colleagues developed a memory test for horses. The horses had to memorise 20 pairs of pictures and identify the symbol which represented food. Once the horses had 'downloaded' this information to their long-term memory, 85 per cent of them were still able to remember the picture pairs correctly after six months. This impressive ability to remember things is comparable to the proverbial memory of elephants.

Conversely, it is usually very difficult for a horse to undo an association, once it has been established. When something that used to be correct for many years is now suddenly wrong by the new owner's standards, the horse will find it very difficult to replace the old association with a new one.

It is amazing what horses will think of – not only as foals.

perfect. In addition, the emotions the horse experiences during the exercises and the information intake are extremely important for the memorisation. We learn best when we are attentive, motivated and relaxed. It can be a lot of fun to motivate a horse, because they are very curious and can grasp surprising associations at their own working pace, which will then remain in their memory for a very long time. It is especially easy to learn and memorise new information that is similar to already known information. Our horse can therefore transfer the signals he learned on the ground to the work under saddle, if our symbolic language remains recognisable.

The Sea of Creativity

There are conspicuous differences in the creativity of different horses. While some horses always move in the same old pathways and hardly try any new movement patterns, others constantly reinvent themselves. We probably all know an 'escape artist', who constantly investigates new parts of the fence to increase his range. And there are many different possibilities of crossing a fence. At first, he may jump it, then crawl underneath it, or flatten it and break it. Those who think that they are a step ahead of their horse by raising or improving the fence often underestimate their 'creative free spirit'. These horses seem to know whether the power is turned on and where the weak spots of the fence are, and they keep trying new ideas of getting to the other side through circus-worthy contortions. There are seemingly no limits to their creativity.

However, creativity is an ability that most riders rarely notice in their horses. Traditional training leaves little or no room for the horse's ideas and creativity. The human sets the task and expects the only 'right' answer. Everything else is ignored, or in the worst case scenario suppressed or punished, although most horses like being creative, from the colt to the retiree. You can see this most impressively when you leave the firmly established pathways and occupy yourself with more creative options, such as playing, clicker training, or circus movements. But even here, only those who allow the horse to unfold its personality will see true inventiveness. Become creative yourself: You don't need to play football if the horse can do it better with its nose. Usually we have a clear idea in our mind of what is 'right', even when we are playing. As children, we let our imagination run much more-freely, and along the same lines we can sometimes let our horse make up a game, too.

For instance, you could simply bring your horse an unknown object that cannot injure the horse – such as a large stuffed animal or a pillow. Wait and see what happens, and play along, without trying to judge 'right' or 'wrong'. Just accompany your horse's path with rewards and praise. One horse may be motivated through rewards to toss the object in the air or to shake it with its mouth. Another will push it around the ground with its nose, or step on it with its hoof. It is especially impressive when you try the same game options with different horses. You will quickly notice the characteristic idiosyncrasies in the inventiveness and creativity of each animal. Some will generally lose interest very quickly and require much encouragement, praise, and treats, while another sees the toy as a welcome diversion and loses itself in trying the many possibilities of the game.

Learning to Learn

Every animal has to protect its brain from an excess of information, impressions, and memories. It has a limited processing capacity and can only absorb a certain amount of information. While some horses are true all-round talents that can be brilliant in many different disciplines with very different tasks, others have very few, or only one, true talent. This is generally caused by a lack of stimulation as a foal. Every horse should learn as early as possible in life, in order to be able to use its brain effectively. As we know, certain connections in the brain have to be developed during childhood. The more connections are established between brain cells, the better the horse will be able to master the tasks that it is faced with. It is consequently necessary to keep the horses busy already as foals with varied individualised and inspiring exercises. Easy leading exercises, the first calmness training, or simple tricks keep the foal occupied and develop its intelligence. The brain can grow and develop only when it is confronted with many different thinking tasks. But varying the exercises places high demands on us humans, too. It is, of course, much easier to ride the same laps around the arena. And it certainly takes some effort to choose toys and take them to the horses. Yet, besides species appropriate accomodation, this is the only possibility to support the processing capacity, and with it the intelligence of our horse.

In-the-Box Thinking

Behavioural scientists use the term 'generalising' in reference to the association of similarities. Initially, a certain stimulus has either a positive or negative association. As a result, the horse can form an idea about this stimulus and respond the same way to similar stimuli. A known phenomenon in this respect is a fear of the vet. The triggering stimulus might be the smell or the visual appearance of the vet in this case. The horse may have endured a painful treatment by a vet, which created a negative association. At first, only the vet in question is considered unpleasant, later on all vets may be classified as dangerous through the process of generalisation, or all men in general, or all humans wearing lab coats ... the horse remembers a specific detail – the gender, the clothing, or the deep voice – and generalises this feature.

There are clever escape artists among horses – the only thing that helps is more occupation and an improvement in the accomodation situation.

This generalisation and the definition of classification criteria in the brain require a certain ability to think and a certain intelligence. When a horse is able to generalise, however, it can most likely also learn to distinguish things and to categorise them. There have been some very interesting research results in this area in recent years. Tests have been conducted about the differentiation and classification of objects. Evelyn B. Hanggi has published some studies under the title The Brain Under The Mane, that received a great deal of attention. She was able to prove that horses can categorise objects according to their consistency (hard or soft), shape (round or square), or colour (blue or yellow). They were able, for instance, to classify the previously unknown sponge as 'soft' or a ball as 'round' by pressing specific buttons on a test apparatus. These intellectual abilities of our horses are truly breathtaking, because they are the equivalent of the developmental stage of a human toddler.

Brain Exercises for Horses

Little brain-teaser exercises are good for horses, too, and they are fun for everyone involved – for instance the popular kid's birthday game 'grab apple'. All we need for it is a large bucket of water. We toss an apple into the water before our horse's eyes. The apple will float on the surface of the water and we have an opportunity to 'watch our horse think'. Our horse will nosily try to grab the apple out of the

If a horse has a negative experience with a veterinarian, it may become suspicious of all humans who look or smell like a veterinarian afterwards.

A little brain teaser: Creativity is required to get a hold of the apple.

water, and find out in the process that this is not so easy. The apple bounces up and down in the water, it disappears beneath the surface, or rolls along the inside of the bucket. Depending on the individual intelligence and character, our horse will try different problem-solving strategies. In this game, there is also no 'right' or 'wrong', because there are very many different ways of getting the apple – and everything goes, whatever it takes. The horse could knock the bucket over with its foot or nose, drink the water, push the apple against the rim of the bucket, or dunk it with its mouth to pin it against

the bottom. Some horses nudge their human repeatedly with their nose, perhaps in the hope of getting help.

Horses possess a quite unique and for us unusual type of intelligence. We humans would be overtaxed in the world of the horse, because only horses possess all those qualities that they need for survival in their natural environment. We would probably have trouble recognising the many different types of grass just by their flavour. It is a different kind of intelligence, that deserves our admiration and appreciation.

Withered Souls

Intelligence and creativity are essential features of a healthy personality - and they suffer from the consequences of inappropriate treatment and a lack of creative outlets. The farther we move away from the nature of the horse, the higher the probability will be that we will have problems with our horse. The less the horse is able to live its basic needs, the more its soul withers away.

Horse owners often don't notice their horse's silent screams until the animal's pathological behaviour bothers them – if the horse starts cribbing not only in the stable, but also tied up in the yard. Or, if it not only pins its ears angrily when the girth is tightened, but actually starts kicking seriously. In order to protect the horse from suffering, we all have to look more closely, because frustration and stress in the horse's life have many faces.

The Basic Rights of Horses

Psychological disorders are reactions to violations of basic needs. Horses strive for orientation in life and have to be able to find their bearings in their living environment. It is therefore important to keep the living conditions as constant as possible or to prepare a horse carefully for new situations. Frequent changes of stables, herds, and caretakers are enormously stressful for horses. A move certainly cannot always be avoided, but one should weigh the pros and cons for the horse very thoroughly.

It has to spend 24 hours of every day in the environment we choose – that's why only the best should be good enough. It is indispensable that all basic needs, from the food to the make-up of the herd and the available space, are as close to nature as possible.

We also give the horse bearings by deciding on a single training method. Consistency means predictability for the horse. What is allowed today should not be forbidden tomorrow. We confuse our horses and make them insecure or even unhappy, if we don't create a familiar

Fresh air, exercise, and interaction with other horses are basic equine needs that need to be met in order for a horse to be happy.

learning environment. Every horse needs the experience of being in control of its own life. Of course, it cannot always decide what it wants to do next in the daily routine with humans. That's why we must motivate our horse, so that it is eager to work with us and so that it has the feeling of being able to make decisions itself. One should be careful with methods that demand an absolute dependency of the animal on the trainer. The animal is severely limited in its self-determination, which will result in a psychological weakening. Creative training methods like clicker training are therefore preferable.

Behavioural Disorders

Like certain zoo animals, some horses show true behavioural disorders. They crib all day, weave from side to side, or mutilate themselves. These are all behaviours that have never been observed to such an unusual degree in 'normal' horses that grew up in the wild. In extreme cases such horses are no longer able to take care of their own wellbeing. They hardly interact with other horses any more, or prefer cribbing to eating. Each of these behavioural disorders probably serves as a coping strategy. The horse views it as a mechanism to reduce an acute state of stress and to escape temporarily into a relaxation phase. This relaxation has a rewarding effect on the horse, so that it will seek this form of relaxation more frequently in the future. The behaviour begins to be self-satisfying.

Initially, it is only a ritual for the horse; later it manifests itself as a true stereotype. Behavioural

Round pen – Anything but Force-Free

What happens in the popular training methods using the round pen? A threatening background is set up to provoke a movement of the horse. Simultaneously, the horse is severely limited in its ability to move by the fence of the round pen. The situation does not leave an escape route and forces the desired reaction. These trainers also use a technique of ignoring, when they are not making any active demands of the animal. Ignoring the horse for long periods of time and applying pressure is the equivalent of mobbing in humans. Initially, these methods may not seem to have negative effects. The horses appear to become affectionate and submissive. They 'function' fantastically. However, there has been no intensification of the bond, but on the contrary a severe loss of the need to bond. We observe an insecure-ambivalent type of bonding in these horses, often a mixture of avoidance, defensiveness, calming signals and freezing. This phenomenon has been described in similar form for humans who have had to live for a long time in a tension field of threat and complete disregard. These human victims would seem without initiative, yet cooperative and paradoxically even showed empathy for their torturers. Horses show these behaviours as well, and feel forced to give up their own personality. That's why the owners have no problems with these horses. But the horses unfortunately have a problem with their life.

Cribbing is a behavioural disorder which serves to reduce stress and is indicative of deficits in either the stabling situation or the handling of the horse.

scientists use the term stereotypes to refer to conspicuous behavioural elements that are shown regularly and continuously in an almost identical form. In most cases, this behaviour does not at all fit the horse's current situation. Some horses even crib, although the other horses are busy playing, and don't always seem to be aware of their environment. The processes in their brain are similar to those of humans suffering from addictions. The addiction or the stereotypical behaviour becomes the dominant life content. As in any form of addiction, the patient seeks 'more'. Stereotypical behaviour in horses becomes more

pronounced over the years as well, if there is no therapy and no improvement in the living conditions. It is caused by a combination of genetics and a species-inappropriate way of stabling the horse. Other contributing factors can be stress, intellectual overtaxing or understimulation, and a suboptimal feeding programme. Many horses that lead a monotonous life with little stimulation develop these behavioural tendencies that make their life a little more bearable. Horses don't copy these behavioural disorders from each other, yet there are often several animals with similar disorders in the same inadequate circumstances. Isolation is another extreme deterioration in the living situation of such a horse. The stress will also increase when it is prevented from using its coping strategy, for instance by having to wear a cribbing collar. Then it usually forms another behavioural disorder – a vicious cycle that can only be broken through an improvement in the living circumstances on all levels. It is likely that such a horse will not stop cribbing entirely, in spite of a change inits living situation, but it will enjoy a much higher quality of life thanks to the improvement in its circumstances.

Pain is one of the most common causes for behavioural problems in horses. Since horses suffer in silence, and since it is so difficult for us humans to gauge their pain, the veterinarian should perform a general check-up whenever there is a behavioural anomaly. Different horses show a wide variety of reactions to pain stimuli. One individual may become restless, the second one introverted and sleepy, or irritable and aggressive. Observations as to which reactions, which body temperature and respiratory frequency are 'normal' for a horse are very helpful for the evaluation of whether it suffers from pain or how intense the pain is. It is not only acute pain, but also chronic pain, which has often been overlooked for years, that can create a change in behaviour. In addition, there is the so-called 'pain memory'. The animal that is affected remembers subconsciously that a certain touch used to cause pain at some point in the past, for instance. If the animal is very sensitive, or if the pain was very intense, merely looking at a certain area of the body

Pain is among the most common causes for behavioural anomalies or rebellious behaviour.

Horses can handle situations of acute stress quite well, just like humans.

If the horse is frequently overtaxed, on the other hand, this leads to chronic stress, which makes the horse sick.

is already enough. It will still react defensively, although the actual pain is long gone, because it had learned this through the painful stimulus. It has now become a habit to flinch, to withdraw, or to threaten.

The Stress is Killing Me!

Stress and frustration are a part of life. Nature doesn't always offer the horse the food and water it needs in abundance without having to work for it. The presence of food competitors also equates to stress, and members of the same species can sometimes get in the way of fulfilling one's own wishes. The unique personality of each individual horse determines which situations are perceived as frustrating or stressful, as well as what the reactions to them look like. The genetic predisposition towards certain stress reactions plays as much a role as the individual life story and learning experiences of each horse.

First of all, the experience of stress is not bad or unnatural per se, but merely an adjustment of the body to various external conditions. The body is put on alert, which enables it to react and to make decision very quickly. In this exceptional situation, a primordial part of the brain, the brain stem, takes control in order to be able to react lightning fast to an unexpected or new situation. The entire body is mobilised within a fraction of a second: The heart rate is increased, the blood sugar level rises, the blood circulation in the musculature increases, and the bronchi are dilated. The 'stress hormone' adrenalin curtails the digestive, growth and renewal processes in the organism, so that all the disposable energy is available for flight or defence.

Chronic stress, on the other hand, leads to harmful changes of the metabolism, and the immune and reproductive systems. In extreme cases, chronic stress makes the animal sick and can lead to severe mental repercussions, such as reduced learning ability or drastically reduced memory, because the horse is no longer psychologically balanced.

Recognising stress in a horse is not always easy. There are active stress types that prance around, nip, or have a tendency to rear. The passive stress types, on the other hand, show behaviours such as freezing and can thus easily appear 'stubborn', 'lazy', or simply unfazed, so that the human likes to believe his horse is laid back and stress-resistant. The problem, however, is that this stress type 'internalises' its worries for a long time, until seemingly all of a sudden it tries to break out of its miserable situation. Every rider should watch the calming signals, such as frequent yawning or the chewing motion, a defensive facial expression, or a lack of ear movement (cf. the explanations on pages 54–60). Certain physical signals, such as a change in respiratory rate, increased sweating, frequent bowel movements, or tense musculature point to an increased stress level as well. If you know your horse well enough, you will develop a sense for how stressed your horse is at the moment.

Horses can suffer short-term frustrations without damage, if they can find solutions and if they have learned to develop problem-solving strategies. They can learn through rewards to leave a four-legged friend for a short time on a hack. In this situation, it is important to present the horse with a task that it already knows well, as an alternative to rushing after the friend. Positive reinforcement during training helps to keep stress levels as low as possible. However, it can still happen from time to time that the horse gets frustrated, because it doesn't see a solution or because it doesn't understand the exercise. Through a clever exercise design and many little experiences of success you can help the horse to overcome its frustration and to enjoy the training.

Strategies against Stress

Changes are just as much potential stress factors for a horse as being chronically challenged too much or too little. Any change in training, in the accomodation situation, and in feeding should therefore be prepared and executed very carefully. A reliable training plan along with an appropriate mental and physical work-out prevents stress as well. It is important to accustom young horses to the outside stimuli of the human world – horse trailers, noise, shows, traffic, and so on – but without flooding them with too many stimuli at one time.

Most importantly, all persons who are - involved in the training of the horse have to support each other and use the same method, give the same signals, and establish clear behavioural rules. Otherwise, the horse cannot find its bearings in its training world.

Living in Balance

In all activities, it is important to find a reasonable measure of the demands for the individual horse. Something that overtaxes one horse can be just right for another one, and vice versa. When the horse is overtaxed, the brain cannot keep up with processing the demands. It becomes overstimulated and sends stress signals to the body. That's why breaks are indispensable for all living beings. This fact is often applied in training only in a physical sense. Most riders react to signs of physical exhaustion, but hardly anybody pays attention to the horse's psychological frame of mind. Glassy eyes and an indifferent attitude, but

Being allowed to be a horse – especially for hard-working show horses, R&R breaks are very important.

also difficulty executing familiar exercises, are all signs of being over-faced.

Being permanently under-challenged is just as unhealthy, if our horses are constantly bored. In nature, boredom is relatively rare, since the horse spends most of its time eating, socialising, and migrating. If the change in living conditions prevents this natural schedule, it creates a gap that has to be filled by other forms of activities. Not only riding, but also taking a walk together, creative ground work or additional pasture time keep the horse busy and fill its life in a positive way.

Learned Helplessness

If a horse experiences being 'limited', 'restricted', or 'punished' very frequently, it enters a state called learned helplessness, in addition to the possible fears and aggressions. The horse becomes increasingly passive and will no longer try to defend itself, even against very negative actions. Instead, it resigns itself to its fate. It has withdrawn into a sense of general helplessness and powerlessness, since its experience has been that its needs and feelings are not being heard, and that it can neither defend itself nor - escape. You can recognise this state usually by the lack of ear movement, the empty stare, and the powerless overall impression. Such horses are often presented by their trainers as especially sweet or well-mannered, and most owners unfortunately see them as 'normal'. The horse has learned that it is not worth it to try anything, and behaves as passively and inconspicuously as possible. In reality, these creatures are being suppressed and live in

Horses that hardly show any outward reactions are not sweet, but in a state of great helplessness.

constant stress and fear. There is a kind of split between the emotions and the experience of the moment. This state is psychological torture for the horse.

The human plays a decisive role in the mental wellbeing of the horse. S/he is intellectually capable of reflecting upon his/her own behaviour and to change the horse's living circumstances for the better. S/he is the one who has to become aware of how s/he wants to keep and treat his/her horse. It's entirely up to the human whether a horse's soul blossoms or withers.

Now we are coming full circle with this book, and we still don't know exactly what it would be like to be a horse. And it appears very unlikely that we will ever find out precisely what it is like, no matter how much we try.

No matter how well informed we are, no matter how many thick books we have read on the subject, and no matter how much time we spend observing, the nature of the horse will always surprise us with new mysteries. And yet, thanks to behavioural biology, we have learned more about equine psychology and emotions in the last few years than during the entire history of this unequal partnership. We can describe their sensory perceptions very accurately today and thereby get an impression of their world. We know that, just like ours, their brain possesses all the structures that are necessary to feel emotions. Horses can be afraid, angry, or happy, and they are able to communicate their desires and fears to us. They may speak a different language, yet their complex way of communication is incredibly fascinating, and with a little understanding it should be possible for us to enter some form of dialogue with them.

Current scientific studies show that we have merely begun to understand the intellectual and creative faculties of horses, and that there are many surprising discoveries to be expected in the future. But our horses can fulfil this mental potential only if we support and develop them properly. Otherwise, it will be our responsibility if they wither away psychologically or become mentally ill. It is in our hands whether our horse is afraid of us and is not allowed to show any

initiative in our presence, or whether we spend our free time with a strong and interesting personality who contributes his own ideas and has his own head. Modern behavioural science clearly confirms the entirely positive character of learning through rewards, and debunks the common learning mechanisms in horse training as pure negative methods. Besides, it is a fallacy to think that an animal is more 'obedient', or easier to handle, when it is being suppressed. On the contrary, it will perform a behaviour that it learned this way only very unwillingly and under pressure, and the pent-up frustration and suppressed aggression can eventually have devastating consequences for both horse and rider.

Anybody who has taught a horse a trick with a treat will know the obvious difference to the pressure method. That's why we should always try to reach our goals in a playful manner, so that our horses are able to understand them. Then they will like coming to us and face the demands of life in human company with a smile, and their entire life will be like a great playground. We are responsible for their wellbeing and the development of their creativity and joy in life. That's why we start developing our horses now, today, even if sometimes we have to put our own wishes on the back-burner. This book can only be a modest suggestion of how we can create a horseworthy living space for every horse, design new games, strengthen their self-confidence and boost the development of their personality with intelligence training and creativity exercises. You horse will show us with its body language and facial expressions what it is thinking and feeling

Appendix

Recommended Reading

• Ball, Stefan:
Emotional Healing For Horses & Ponies
CW Daniel, 2001

• Coates, Margrit: *Horses Talking ·
How to Share Healing Messages with
the Horses in Your Life*
Rider, 2005

• Fisher, Sarah: *Know Your Horse Inside Out:*
A Clear, Practical Guide to Understanding
and Improving Posture and Behaviour
David & Charles, 2009

• Rashid, Mark: *Horses Never Lie:*
The Heart of Passive Leadership
David & Charles, 2004

Contact the author

www.pferdsein.de: Marlitt Wendt's
homepage with information on the
subject of equine behaviour and
creative horse training and with offers
of seminars in behavioural biology.

Index

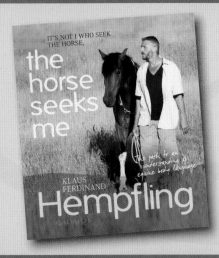
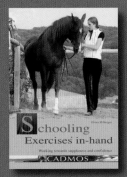
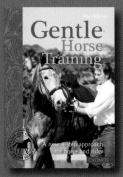